DON'T PAINT YOUR KITCHEN

HOW TO SELL YOURSELF
& GET THE JOB YOU WANT

JOEY HIMELFARB

Don't Paint Your Kitchen
How to Sell Yourself & Get the Job You Want
Copyright© 2022 by Joey Himelfarb
First Edition Copyright© 2017

ISBN: 979-8-9865812-0-0

Printed in the United States of America

Published by Joey Himelfarb

Cover Design: Eric Labacz, www.labaczdesign.com
Cover photo and other photos of Joey by Laura Pedrick, https://www.pedrickphoto.com/

To Lennon

From the day you arrived and blinked into the sun, the Circle of Life continues with you, little lady.

CONTENTS

INTRODUCTION

How many psychiatrists does it take to change a light bulb?
Just one…but the light bulb has to want to change.

When I was let go from my corporate position in sales, I was afforded the opportunity to make use of the resources of an outplacement company. After my outplacement stint was complete, it was suggested that I start attending networking groups. Up until that moment (mid-2003) I had never used networking and groups in the same sentence. I didn't know what they were. Today, in 2022, these groups are all over the place, but back then, they were few and far between.

As it was explained to me, these groups, composed primarily of unemployed professionals, meet regularly: weekly, biweekly, or monthly. Typically, these gatherings take place at a public location such as a library, a church, or a synagogue. Some businesses will open their own conference rooms for these groups. These job seekers gather to provide support and offer guidance and direction to each other during their period of unforeseen or unwanted transition.

In addition, speakers with different backgrounds are traipsed in meeting after meeting to teach the group things to help everyone land their next job. Topics of discussion might be how to write a resume, how to research a company, how to dress for an interview—technical-type stuff.

The networking group I was referred to was highly recommended. Meetings occurred every Tuesday evening for two hours at a YMCA about thirty minutes from home so I decided to check it out.

My life changed in so many ways because of the Career Forum at the Somerset Hills Y in Basking Ridge, New Jersey. The people I met who supported me, and vice versa, were from all walks of life. Bob, Lloyd, and Denis (may he rest in peace) are responsible for helping me break new ground by offering me a platform to share my experience and expertise. You could say they indirectly had a hand in the development and creation of this book. Thank you, gentlemen!

I soon came to discover the attendees at these meetings were out of work for periods ranging anywhere from two days to two months. Sometimes even two years.

Some of the participants were recent college graduates looking for assistance to find their first job. Some were experienced professionals from various industries such as healthcare, finance, hospitality, retail, and construction. And some folks were returning to the job market after being away for years.

All of them identified as their last title—marketer, accountant, product manager, auto mechanic, customer service representative, computer programmer—or role—caregiver, student, mom, dad, professional in transition.

Over time, as we got to know each other, it became

clear that most of us, including yours truly, were anxious and slightly concerned about our futures. Some people were sad and clearly worried. A select few were downright despondent, totally frustrated, pissed at the world, and ready to punch their fist through a wall. Or into a hiring manager's face if a job was not being offered.

One night while waiting for a meeting to begin, several of us were chatting about our job searches in particular and our lives in general. As I heard more and more negative and downtrodden comments surfacing among the crowd, I stopped the conversation midstream and said: "I've been selling for many years and have learned to embrace a positive and upbeat attitude, and to surround myself with people who demonstrate that attribute as well. I need to be around Positive Paulas and Gung-ho Garys, not Negative Nellies and Toxic Tonys.

"Secondly, I'm not clairvoyant, but if you maintain this defeatist mindset and continue to lay blame for your current plight at the world's feet, you're gonna be here next year still looking for work. You are not doing a good job of selling yourself."

Well, while they stood there stunned by my diatribe and transfixed by my soapbox delivery, I had an epiphany. ***Looking for your next job IS selling yourself.***

My experiences in selling, which continue every day, have taught me there is a science to selling but there is also definitely an art. Ask P.T. Barnum or Ron Popeil. Just know there are tried and true ways to sell effectively and definitely ways NOT to sell. We will explore them both.

For now, I contend that your quest to find meaningful work and land your next dream job are directly related to how successful you are at selling yourself.

You see, I love to sell, and I love to teach. I thrill for the opportunity to be on a stage, present information, facilitate a conversation, and influence an audience hungry for knowledge. It's an indescribable feeling watching proverbial light bulbs turning on over people's heads while leading a conversation. Actually, I can describe it. *It's fantastic! Cathartic! Satisfying! Rewarding! Fulfilling!*

Anyway, in that split second, I realized I could be one of those speakers who present to these groups. So during that meeting and the half-hour drive home, I formulated an outline in my mind of a presentation I thought might resonate with this group.

At home, I quickly did a brain dump by typing my thoughts into a brief description of my idea for a presentation. The next day I reached out to the group's moderator and shared my idea for presenting "Selling Yourself." I suggested making this presentation once or twice and then slinking back into the audience. It would be my contribution to everyone.

"Sure thing, Joey. We're always looking for new blood and would welcome your contribution," he said.

So off I went and worked on developing and creating a sixty-minute presentation that extrapolates the art and science of selling to the job search process. What you are about to read is a collection of some of the concepts I've shared with networking groups over the years, and still do. I'll be sharing with you how I believe selected parts of the job search process can be likened to the process of selling—theoretically, conceptually, and creatively.

I've successfully facilitated these strategies and tactics

with college students, unemployed professionals, and others who have returned to the job market. I hope to do the same for you and help you land your dream job sooner than expected with minimal stress and strife.

At the end of each chapter I've included action items for you to think about and/or complete. Some are simple; others not so much; they will demand introspection and require deep thought. All are suggested to help put you in the mindset of a successful salesperson.

Take your time going through these activities. There are no time limits, per se, nor are there right or wrong responses. There is no answer guide at the back of the book. Whatever you feel makes sense to you at the time is correct. Let your gut be your guide—it hardly ever lets you down.

Completing these activities will better prepare you for the individual tasks that combine to achieve the overall objective of finding your next job, perhaps your dream job. Please suspend all thoughts of you as a job seeker. Instead, imagine you are a salesperson tasked with closing your next sale.

Remember, looking for a job is selling yourself. Let's work to make you the knight in shining armor that the hiring manager has been looking for. If she offers you a position on her team and wonders where you've been all this time, and why it's taken so long for the two of you to get together, then you've succeeded.

Onward and upward.

CHAPTER 1
PUT ON YOUR SALES HAT

We see our customers as invited guests to a party, and we are the hosts. It's our job every day to make every important aspect of the customer experience a little bit better.

—*Jeff Bezos*

SELLING IS...

If you agree with me that looking for work is akin to selling yourself, then let's define what selling is so we can operate from the same script.

At the beginning of my seminar entitled "Selling Yourself," I lead a quick exercise and ask the audience to let me know what activities they think are used by salespeople to sell. My only prompt is "Selling is dot, dot, dot. How would you complete that phrase?"

I don't give them any hints or clues as to what should be included in this list. It's theirs to create. I'm their scribe. I write their responses on a whiteboard or easel so everyone can see them. Or I'll capture their input onscreen if the seminar is being delivered online. Regardless of the medium, everyone can see the list.

Participation swells and the list grows as audience members share their opinions of what they believe selling is. I don't judge their input. I might ask for clarification or request they summarize an extensive thought or idea. The total wisdom of the group is captured in a collection of verbs and nouns. Simple. Easy to understand. Relatable. This is a small sampling of the responses I've received over the years:

- Helping customers
- Demonstrating products
- Negotiating prices
- Answering questions
- Listening to customers
- Creating urgency to make a purchase
- Handling objections
- Influencing decisions
- Uncovering concerns
- Building relationships
- Asking questions about customer wants and/or needs

WE ARE ALL SALESPEOPLE

When everyone is in agreement that their list is somewhat comprehensive and representative of what salespeople do, I ask how many members in the audience have experience selling. Typically, less than ten percent raise their hands. I expect that. Then I ask how many have been on a job interview, and practically everyone raises their hand.

This is when I sheepishly suggest that they've all sold, maybe not successfully, but they have sold. That statement generates half-hearted giggles so I let those giggles sink in. I want everyone to grasp the concept that we sell every day.

I use this moment to point out an important lesson to be learned, not to be taken lightly. I turn everyone's attention to the sales activities list, their list, and pose these rhetorical questions to the group:

- Aren't these some, if not all, of the things you do during a job interview?
- If you stretch your imaginations a little and substitute hiring managers for customers in the list above, can you see how you are selling yourself, as a product and service, during a job interview?

Invariably, the yeas outnumber the nays. Now I have a room full of unemployed professionals who are on their way to believing they are salespeople. I usually need the next fifty minutes to help get them over the hump of disbelief, but it's not difficult. I suggest they suspend their belief while we're together and imagine themselves as salespeople, NOT job seekers looking for work.

Of course, I'm faced with some trepidation and uneasiness from a few folks but getting everyone to think they're salespeople puts them in a different frame of mind. Doing this, I believe, better prepares them for the daunting task of finding and landing their next job. In order to define what selling is and is not, let's refer to the list of responses on the previous page; it's a concise description of the activities that capture the essence of selling.

SELLING IS PROBLEM SOLVING

If you ask twenty-five people to define selling, you'd probably get twenty-five different answers. ***In my opinion, selling is synonymous with solving problems.*** Problems that people have, struggles that challenge them, and roadblocks that impede their progress. Hassles.

Providing solutions that alleviate, minimize, or remove any or all those hassles is what selling is and what clients want. Anything that doesn't meet or exceed a client's expectations means falling short of serving the client. Based on my experience, these are the tenets I've learned to embrace that capture the essence of selling:

- Selling is serving your clients unconditionally with no strings attached.
- Selling is behaving authentically by being genuinely concerned for your client's success.
- Selling demands being all in regarding every aspect of the solution presented.

If I can get you to treat hiring managers as prospects and clients and consider yourself their salesperson, I believe you will see your job search in a different light. After you read about Oscar in the next chapter, you will see what I mean.

I contend that we sell every day regardless of our status in life or our position in the workforce. You could argue we've been doing so since the Garden of Eden (if you believe in that sort of thing). We sell to our families, friends, and neighbors. We sell to our doctors, hairstylists, auto mechanics, landscapers, accountants. They sell to us. We sell our ideas, suggestions, and opinions. So do they. All. The. Time.

When you post something on social media, you are effectively selling yourself. You don't know who is going to read your post, but it might be your next boss. Or it might be someone you know who introduces you to your next boss. It might even be someone you DON'T know who introduces you to your next boss. It might be someone you don't know who introduces you to someone you don't know who introduces you to your next boss. You don't know. The possibilities are endless.

IT'S NOT WHAT YOU KNOW

The age-old adage—it's not what you know, but who you know—takes on so much more meaning and relevance when you are looking for work. Depending upon which survey you read from which decade, anywhere from fifty to eighty percent of job seekers land jobs that were never advertised or published. It turns out someone knew someone who knew someone at a company somewhere that needed those job seekers. Sometimes the job seekers don't even know the hiring managers they meet. If it wasn't for the extended network those job seekers cultivated and tended to over the years, they'd continue to be unemployed.

Just know that what you're putting out there is some reflection of you, your personality, your character. You. How you present yourself can be critical in helping you land your next position.

I've told both my sons, now in their late twenties and

early thirties, since the days they were born, to be nice to people. I emphasized that you don't know who they might introduce you to one day because of your concern for them. Or how they might NOT help you because you were mean, belligerent, or nasty to them. You just don't know who knows who.

It's a big planet, but Disney was right: It's a small world.

ACTION ITEMS

- List additional activities that you feel salespeople perform that job seekers must do. Think of salespeople you've dealt with. What are some of the things they did with you? For you? To you? When was the last time you were successfully "sold" something? What worked? Why did you buy? What didn't they do that you wished they did? Going through this exercise will help you think like a salesperson. You want to take on the persona of someone who helps others. Doing this will differentiate you from the other job seekers that don't do this. Hiring managers will notice that distinction.

- Create a list of people you know in general—friends, neighbors, family members, service providers. Cull through this list to identify which people you know that work and meet with lots of other people. For example, your doctors and dentist have patients, your dry cleaner and hairstylist have clients, and so do your accountant, banker, lawyer, and realtor. You're looking to connect with referral networkers.

- Review your LinkedIn connections. Who knows who? Who can you assist in their work or job search if they're looking? Who haven't you talked to in a while? Who will you reconnect with? Spend time every day deliberately reconnecting with your world of contacts.

- Update your presence on social media sites including photos and profiles.

- Read *Mindset* by Carol Dweck.

CHAPTER 2
SELLING IS HELPING

You can succeed best and quickest by helping others to succeed.

—*Napoleon Hill*

Let me tell you about Oscar (not his real name). I met Oscar at a networking event. He was a C-level executive with a wealth of knowledge and experience, and a far-reaching network typical of someone with his background. He had all the right boxes checked and possessed all the requisite skills, abilities, and talents needed to excel in his industry.

At the time we met, Oscar had been out of work for almost a year. He was frustrated because he had gone on so many interviews and been rejected one after another. With all that he had going for him, Oscar could not figure out why it was taking so long to land his next gig. After more than eleven months of researching companies, updating his resume ad nauseam, wordsmithing his cover letters, anticipating challenging interview questions, and writing well-thought-out and sincere thank you notes, he was no better off than the day he was let go.

Oscar had a sense that he might have been groveling too much with prospective hiring managers. He thought that perhaps he had practically been begging to be hired by them. His Monday morning quarterbacking also suggested that maybe he wasn't doing a good job of explaining how he could be of value to a company. You can imagine how frustrated Oscar must have felt to be unemployed for all this time with no prospects in sight.

But wait.

Oscar had a plan.

SEE IT. BELIEVE IT. THEN ACT AS IF.

Instead of going to his next interview and asking for a job, he decided to take on the role of a consultant and offer suggestions to help the organization. What did he have to lose? He didn't have a job to start with so not getting hired meant he didn't lose something he didn't have. I'll admit it's a little convoluted, but it kept Oscar sane so more power to him.

Sure enough, when his next interview was scheduled, our man of the hour *acted as if* the people in the room were his clients and he was their account manager selling HIS services. Acting as if better prepares you for the task at hand and helps enhance your confidence. Acting as if is also one of the most effective, surefire ways to manifest something out of nothing—but that's a whole other topic for a whole other book.

Oscar had studied their 10-K report beforehand. In the

interview he asked them about their business and validated some of the challenges he had already concluded that they faced. He then went on to describe scenarios he had dealt with in the past that were similar to the scenarios these individuals said were occurring at their company presently. With that understanding in place, Oscar then shared in elaborate detail how he helped solve manufacturing problems, alleviated personnel issues, and reduced supply chain inefficiencies in his previous positions.

Oscar felt the interview went well and took their "we'll get back to you in about two weeks because we have other candidates to interview" as a sign that he might be invited back. After eleven months of this grueling job-hunting process, he was feeling almost numb and slightly beaten up. Regardless, he knew a positive and optimistic mindset was better than the alternative.

He was invited back a week later and met again with the same people he had interviewed previously. When he sat down in the conference room, they handed him a thirty-seven-page document.

"Oscar, when you were here last you asked a lot of questions about our business and you were kind enough to share with us your thoughts, ideas, and suggestions for helping us get better at what we do. The document you have in your hands is a summary of what you shared with us. If these are the strategies and tactics you used in your previous life at other companies to solve their problems, then we'd like you to implement them here for us, too."

Oscar started working with these people soon thereafter.

A PARABLE

I share Oscar's story because it reminds me of the parable about searching for happiness. Here's the Cliffs Notes version; Happiness is like a butterfly. When you chase it, even with the largest net you can carry, the butterfly will always elude you. However, if you ignore the butterfly and go about your day, lo and behold, the butterfly will come to rest lightly on your shoulder when you least expect it.

I know it's a little woo-woo and New Age sounding. However, I think with regards to you and your job search, chasing your next job, let alone begging and groveling for it, is both demanding and tiring. The rejections alone could drive you into a tailspin and down a rabbit hole.

If left unchecked, it can be difficult to reverse the feelings of despair you may feel as you receive rejection after rejection. As time marches on and the rebuffs mount, you might start to feel unimportant, unwanted, unworthy. All these "un"s could start to take a toll on your psyche, as it did for Oscar. If you don't nip these negative feelings in the bud, you run the risk of becoming indolent, crabby, incorrigible, and bitter. All that negativity enters your bones and muscles—the very essence of you and your DNA.

Soon you're pissed at the world and, although you started this process with good intentions just like Dr. Henry Jekyll, your demeanor nosedives and you become Mr. Edward Hyde.

Not approachable. Not attractive. Scary. Frightening.

Who would want to talk to you? Would you? Who

would want to help you? You know you wouldn't want to help yourself so why would someone else want to?

BECOME A CONSULTANT

That's why I suggest you think of yourself as a consultant, a provider of solutions to problems. In other words, a salesperson. If you genuinely envision yourself as a knight in shining armor who comes to save the day for the company with which you are interviewing, a few things will happen:

- You won't feel compelled to beg or grovel.
- The pressure to land your next job is off.
- Your customer, the hiring manager, might be more forthcoming and share additional details about obstacles they're facing in hopes that you can help overcome them.

In Sales Training 101, an important lesson is taught: ***People don't like to be sold to, but they do love to buy from.*** In other words, if you feel a salesperson has pushed something onto you without any concern for your best interests or regard for your well-being or forced you to hand over your money for their stuff, then chances are great you won't freely brag to friends and family about the wonderful purchase you have made.

On the other hand, if the salesperson makes the effort to better understand what you're all about and what you truly want and/or need, then you'll willingly buy from said Superhero in a cape. How salespeople learn to better understand their clients is another lesson from Sales Training 101, which we'll address in the next chapter.

SKILLS, ABILITIES, TALENTS

If you live in the United States, I'm sure you're familiar with the SATs. The Scholastic Aptitude Test used to be the minimum de facto exam every high school senior had to slog through and score high on for colleges and universities to even consider them for admission. In this post-COVID world, the SATs are going the way of fax machines and iPods, slowly disappearing from the landscape.

I would like to repurpose the acronym and hope you will as well as you continue to look for your next job. Begin to think of the acronym SAT as the ***skills, abilities, and talents*** that make each of you unique. As a job seeker, your job is to demonstrate to prospective hiring managers how you can help them and their organizations. By bringing your SATs to bear, these hiring managers will see how you can help them become stronger, faster, and leaner than their competition.

SELLING YOUR SATS

Here's where you sell your SATs so hiring managers can learn what you can do. These overworked, over-stressed, and underpaid (don't ask them about it, but you know they think they are not being paid their worth) hiring managers want evidence that you can take on some of their work and relieve some of their stress.

Show them what you did somewhere yesterday you

can do for them at their company today and tomorrow.

I suggest, as you go about looking for work, you take on the role of a consultant, just as Oscar did. Be a problem solver. A solution provider. Be a salesperson. Tout your SATs. Shout them from the rooftops as no one else can. Even though your parents would gladly do it for you, the selling must come from you.

ACTION ITEMS

- Ask friends, family, neighbors, and people you've worked with to help you identify and list your skills, abilities, and talents. What are you good at? What can you do exceptionally well? What special aptitudes do you have that others would pay you for?

- Google *Dave Packard's 11 Simple Rules* and read this short, one-page document. It was written by Dave Packard, one of the founders of the Hewlett-Packard Company, HP. He presented it during a company meeting in 1958. Dave shares excellent guidance and timeless instructions on how to treat people with dignity and respect. If you want to land your next job, you HAVE to treat everyone you meet and connect with as you would like to be treated. It's Dave's elaboration on the Golden Rule.

- Take on the role of a helper as you meet administrative assistants, receptionists, and hiring managers. They are all busy dealing with things that you are not aware of. Imagine yourself as a salesperson showing up to help, not as a job seeker looking for work. This is a subtle distinction but a huge difference in your approach to humanely helping people while you genuinely sell yourself!

- Remember, looking for a job is selling yourself. Therefore, when you're doing anything related to your job search such as researching companies, requesting informational interviews, attending networking events, writing cover letters, updating your resume, meeting with hiring managers, or writing thank-you notes, keep your chin up and chest out, put on a big smile, and get your bright eyes shining. No one wants to deal with, or help, a sourpuss.

- For a lighthearted reprieve from your job search, check out this clip of Robert's Interview from Everybody Loves Raymond[1]: ELR-Robert's Interview https://www.youtube.com/watch?v=UKJTOBNb1mg.

---

[1] *Everybody Loves Raymond*, Philip Rosenthal.

CHAPTER 3
BE THE SOLUTION, NOT THE PROBLEM

If you're not with us, you're against us.
—Gaston to Belle, Beauty and the Beast

Ten thousand years ago in a previous life I used to sell swimming pools. People would see our "pool under construction" signs on front lawns where pools were being built and call the 800 phone number to request a sales consultation.

A salesperson, yours truly, would be given one of these leads and travel to these prospects' homes to teach them the process of what it takes to design, build, and maintain a residential swimming pool. When I knocked on a prospect's door, it wasn't a random knock on a random door in a random neighborhood because I had nothing to do that day. The homeowners knew why I was there, and so did I. But just showing up did not guarantee the sale was a done deal. I had to sell the concept of owning a concrete swimming pool. More importantly, I had to sell myself.

Allow me to elaborate.

After knocking on the prospect's door, making the

necessary introductions, and getting past the pleasantries, I would sit at the kitchen or dining room table with my prospect and pull out a pad of paper and pen. Instead of dumping literature and multiple samples of tile and brick in front of these folks, I would proceed to ask a series of questions. These simple questions were designed to get the prospects thinking about ALL the aspects of pool ownership. While questions and answers went back and forth like a volleyball over a net, we were creating and designing some THING for their backyard that was appropriate for their needs, wants, desires, and lifestyle. Not mine. Theirs.

WE HAVE WAYS OF MAKING YOU TALK

Why are you getting a pool? Why are you getting a pool now? What are you gonna do with this pool? Is it for exercise? Recreation? Are you going to play volleyball in the shallow end? Entertainment? Are you building this pool so it's something that you can look at when you come home from work at night?

Do you want a deep end? Just so you know, you have to have an eight-foot minimum water depth wherever you install a diving board. Do you want a diving board? Do you need a diving board?

Do you want to heat the pool?

How are you going to disinfect the pool water? Will you use chlorine tablets? Will you use liquid chlorine? Will you use a chlorine generator in conjunction with added salt?

Do you want a spa?

Who lives in the house? Any senior citizens? Infants or small children? Anybody with a physical disability?

One prospect stopped me during our question-and-answer session and said emphatically, "You know, Joey, unless I trust you, I'm not buying anything from you." To which I responded without batting an eye, "I know, Bill. That's the first sale. If you don't trust me, I can't even give away any of this stuff. The reason I'm asking you all these questions is that I don't know you or your family and I want you to trust me. If you do, and you buy into this process, we're gonna come here with some very big and very heavy construction equipment and destroy your backyard. It is going to look like a war zone. But when we're done you're gonna have a beautiful looking pool. And when your friends and family are sitting around that beautiful looking pool, I'm sure they will ask, 'Bill, where did you get this beautiful looking pool?' What do you think I want you to say to them, Bill?" Bill nodded in understanding and said, "Call Joey. Here's his number. Be prepared, though—he is going to ask you a ton of questions."

I received a handful of referrals from Bill's friends and neighbors. Not a ton. A handful. But certainly, more than I ever would have received if I cared more about my commission check than Bill and his family.

IT'S NOT ROCKET SCIENCE

You might think selling swimming pools is not similar to finding your dream job, but I would disagree, respectfully. Finding your dream job IS like selling swimming pools—kind of. You have to sell yourself. And the irony about selling yourself is that it's not about you. It's about them. Your prospect. Or if you're looking for work, the hiring manager. And until they know and trust you, they don't care about you. Even after they know and trust you, they STILL may not care about you. There are exceptions to this rule but know that they care more about themselves and their job first. Not you, my humble job seeker. Not you. Them. (If you were on a stage with a hiring manager, the spotlight would be on them, not you.)

They don't care if you're unemployed, how many bills you have, how many children you're responsible for, how many boyfriends you have, how many wives you have, or how many homes or cars you own. Unless you embezzled funds from your previous employer or hurt one of your ex-employees, this overworked and underpaid hiring manager does not care about you.

All they care about is themselves and the trials and tribulations that stress them out during the day. And let's not forget the nagging feelings and recurring negative thoughts that keep them awake at night. To paraphrase my friend Lloyd, "all they care about are the hassles on their back." If you can demonstrate your ability to make those hassles disappear, then you're in a better position compared to those who cannot.

You have to sell yourself to them. You have to discuss what you did somewhere else yesterday that is applicable in their world today and tomorrow. If you buy into that philosophy and scenario, then we're on our way to helping you help them.

You've been a customer. How do you want to be

treated? Remember when you were the center of attention and your opinions were heard and respected? Be like the salesperson who made you feel good. It's not rocket science but even rocket scientists can benefit from this mindset and philosophy.

Don't be arrogant. Don't be a know-it-all. Don't be the rotten apple that spoils the whole bunch.

Build trust. Cultivate solutions, not problems. Be part of the solution, not the problem. Watch what happens.

DEMONSTRATE YOUR PROBLEM-SOLVING SKILL

Let's assume twenty-five applicants are vying for the position you want. In the job market, you'd be lucky if it's twenty-five. It'll probably be more like 125, possibly 525. How will you stand out from that crowd?

You have to demonstrate that the problems the target company is facing today and tomorrow are problems you managed yesterday somewhere else. You must quantify specific results, with actual numbers, as much as possible on your resume, your LinkedIn profile (you have a LinkedIn profile, right!?), and your cover letters.

It's not enough to provide a bullet list of activities you've performed over the years; everybody does that so nobody stands out. You HAVE to show quantifiable numbers to distinguish yourself from your competition.

Here's a good litmus test to ensure you're distinguishing yourself from the competition: Assume everything you include in your resume and your LinkedIn profile (it's up and public now, right!?) is being questioned by the reader with these two words: ***So what?***

So what, you generated revenue? So what, you minimized expenses? So what, you managed a team? So what, you reduced effort? So what?

Does your resume or LinkedIn profile address those questions and concerns? Yes? Great! The quantifiable results you present are the results the hiring manager wants as well. Sharing those accomplishments explicitly is critical if you want to raise your standing and leave the competition in the dust. Otherwise, if you do not answer those questions or address the reader's skepticism, then your resume is headed for the graphic of a trash can on the computer screen or the circular file under their desk. Consequently, the rest of your LinkedIn profile will be ignored. Thanks for playing. Here's the door. See ya. And no, there are no parting gifts for you. Buh-bye!

Do you see the futility on your part if specific and quantifiable results are NOT included with the list of activities on your resume? Make sure you explicitly answer the questions in the hiring manager's head:

- How much revenue did you generate? $5,000? $5,000,000? In what timeframe? 2 weeks? 2 months? 2 years?
- How many expenses did you minimize? $400? $40,000? $4,000,000? Over how much time? A day? 7 Weeks? 2 Quarters? 9 Months? 3 Years?
- How many people did you manage? 3? 30? 300? 3,000? Were they local, remote, or spread across the country? Or globe?
- How much time (days, weeks, months) and effort (10%, 30%, 75%, 100%) did you remove from processes and

procedures to improve efficiencies, reduce costs, and improve customer retention?

Be specific. While you're meeting with the hiring manager, she is thinking to herself, can this applicant help us? One way you can help her answer that question is by demonstrating your past successes and achievements as specifically as possible with quantifiable results, as they relate to her issue at hand.

ACTION ITEMS

- Check your ego at the door. This is about them, not you. Yes, you want to sell yourself, but not before you demonstrate your genuine concern for, and understanding of, the hiring manager.

- Prepare questions that will help you with answers to better understand the position you're applying for and the company culture. Make sure you've done enough research to uncover as much as you can.

- Review your resume, LinkedIn profile, and social media presence. Ensure every bullet item under your experience contains a problem you solved, an action you undertook, and a quantifiable outcome resulting from that action.

CHAPTER 4
DO YOUR HOMEWORK

Be prepared.

—Boys Scouts of America

Before you go to your interview, you need to do some homework. The obvious place to start is to check out the company where you will be interviewing. Scan their website. Read industry articles and reviews about the company. Search for recent press releases and check out their presence on social media—including Twitter and Facebook.

- What is their business?
- How do they make money?
- What risks does the company face from its industry? From the marketplace? From the competition?
- Who is their competition?
- What are the hassles that the hiring manager is fighting off? And how can you get those hassles off the boss's plate, radar, and to-do list?

WALK BEFORE YOU RUN

Less obvious, but just as important, is knowing yourself. Your ability to describe what you can do and how you can do it is critical to your advancement through the job search process.

What you can do and how you can do it are determined by you because of the homework you do on yourself first. Long before you start looking outward for positions to apply to and companies to work for, you need to look inward. You must do a personal assessment:

- Review where you've been.
- Establish where you are.
- Decide where you're going.

It's such an important part of your job search campaign that you should do this first before you do anything else. Doing so will better prepare you as you search for your dream job. The more thorough your self-assessment, the more focused your job search campaign will be. The more focused you are, the more you will become a lean, mean, job-seeking missile expending minimal energy and saving valuable time. Otherwise, you could be focusing on the wrong positions in the wrong organizations at the wrong companies.

We'll get into more detail about your assessment in our next chapter. Just know many job seekers have had their searches derailed and upended because they didn't take the time to become introspective.

Even though you might be able to demonstrate what

you know, that's not enough. In my humble opinion, I believe that as much as hiring managers care what you know, ***they really want to know that you care.***

I am not belittling your multiple advanced degrees from numerous prestigious institutions or the thirty-six Microsoft classes you've attended and passed or your mastery of the Google Suite. Heck, if you can configure a router while suspended underwater with both hands tied behind your back and blindfolded, more power to you.

If there's a hiring manager who needs that combination of skills in their employee, then you're golden. But NOT if you are NOT a nice person or if you are someone who nobody wants to work with. If you are a bad apple, no hiring manager in their right mind is going to bring you into their fold to spoil the whole bunch of good apples that all get along in peace and harmony.

When it comes to winning over people, Dale Carnegie instructed us to be interested in the other person first, and then be interesting to them.[2] According to Carnegie, the order is critical if you want to win friends and influence people. In other words, get to know THEM before you bombard them with YOU.

I know, I know. During a job interview you have limited time and don't want to spend precious minutes learning about them. You want to get up on your soapbox and shout out, "Here I am!"

Don't do that.

It's in the interview that you want to dig deeper into the things you discovered from your research about this

---

[2] *How to Win Friends and Influence People*, Dale Carnegie.

company. Please don't ask about things you could have learned about them by reviewing their website or reading their 10-K (a comprehensive report filed annually by publicly traded companies; it is required by the U.S. Securities and Exchange Commission). This report contains much more detail than a company's annual report, which is sent to its shareholders before an annual meeting. You should become familiar with the standard sections of the 10-K that describe the company. Remember, it's not about you. It's about them.

As a job seeker, it is better to offer suggestions for solving some of the issues they're dealing with regarding competition, industry pressures, and customer attrition. Even though you'll uncover these things from your research, it behooves you to ask one or two specific questions about these issues to demonstrate that you've done your homework. Your intention is to receive additional information about these issues so you can then elaborate on how you tackled similar problems somewhere else in the past.

There are plenty of sources of information to help you better understand companies and the role for which you're interviewing. Your favorite search engine is a good place to start, asking for links to learn about a company.

ACTION ITEMS

- Read *How to Win Friends and Influence People* by Dale Carnegie.
- Locate some 10-K reports to become familiar with the kind of information that public companies report about their businesses.
- Use the information you read about to develop well-thought-out and relevant questions you can use in your interviews.

CHAPTER 5
THE ART AND SCIENCE OF SELLING (KNOW WHERE YOU ARE GOING)

*If you don't know where you're going
how will you know when you get there?*
—*Yogi Berra*
*If you don't know where you're going
then any road will get you there.*
—*George Harrison*

Like all things complex, there is a science to selling. There is also an art but, most definitely, a rhyme and reason behind what makes some salespeople successful while others struggle to close a sale.

Napoleon Hill in his bestselling book, *Think and Grow Rich*, states that the one quality for success is a **definiteness of purpose**, the knowledge of what one wants, and a burning desire to possess it.[3] Successful salespeople have a vision to be someone, to do something, or to have something. With regards to selling, that translates to quantifiable things such as how many:

---

[3] *Think and Grow Rich*, Napoleon Hill.

- Prospects you want to contact
- Prospects you want to meet
- Contracts you want to sign
- Widgets, or thingamajigs you want to sell

By specifically quantifying what they want to achieve, these salespeople establish targets. These targets then create behaviors, or non-behaviors, for the salespeople to perform to attain those goals. An added benefit of establishing targets is that distractions become less distracting. Some of these distractions aren't even seen, felt, or acknowledged.

It's the laser beam focus that keeps these people on task as the world around them tries to derail them. A friend texts a cat video, email newsletters beg for attention, and laundry piles multiply waiting to be washed, dried, folded, or put away.

They would be lucky if these were the only things trying to break their concentration. But there is also the pile of bills to be paid, the never-ending errands that seem to multiply like rabbits, and the ever-present, energy-depleting, incessant breaking news stories. Amazingly, goals are checked off to-do lists considering all the "stuff" that is swirling around our lives.

WHERE ATTENTION GOES, ENERGY FLOWS

It is the quantifiable and desired outcomes established ahead of time that help keep successful salespeople on track. In their quest to accomplish these goals, distractions are brushed aside, and failed attempts are added to the list of lessons learned. Sometimes one step forward, two steps back is the dance of successful salespeople as they strive to get to where they want to be. They know where they are headed and might even lose sight of the finish line. But they know it's out there. Their attention to their destination keeps them on the path to glory. Depending upon the goal, it could take days, weeks, or years to get there. Larry King, the world-famous radio personality and broadcaster, believed every setback was a step forward. Truer words could not be used to keep a salesperson on track—or a job seeker focused on landing their next dream job.

How does all this extrapolate to you, the job seeker? As George Harrison wrote, "If you don't know where you're going, then any road will get you there.[4]" I suggest that as a job seeker, you don't have the time, the extra money, or the need to expend any more effort than necessary to land your next job. By thinking about and then writing down as many specific details of your dream job, you'll be better prepared to look for it and not be distracted by everything the world is throwing in your way.

Think about the blinders worn by racehorses. There is only one goal for these racehorses—the finish line. Jockeys know the horses can be easily distracted by their competitors, hence the blinders. I am not suggesting that job seekers are like racehorses. No, wait, I am. Keep all the distractions around you at bay by not giving them any more attention than they deserve. Stay focused on your goal of landing your dream job…YOUR dream job. Not any job, your dream job.

Most job seekers, when asked what they are looking

---

[4] *Any Road*, George Harrison.

for, typically respond with "a job." The problem with that response and attitude is that it's not specific enough. In almost every community, in almost any job market, there are jobs for the asking. Depending upon when you're reading this, there can be tens of thousands of unfilled jobs waiting to be snagged. However, these jobs may not be the ones that you want.

In your job search, your desire is not just to find a job; you want to find YOUR dream job. And that will require you to focus your time, attention, and effort to find it. In the famous words of the celebrated American philosopher Yogi Berra, "If you don't know where you're going, how will you know when you get there?"

YOU'LL SEE IT WHEN YOU BELIEVE IT

Exactly. How will you know? Unless you decide specifically what you want to do, you won't know when you have accomplished it. I suggest you take the time to consider the following questions related to your dream job:

- **Why** do you want to do this dream job? Do you want to analyze data? Is it because you like to manage projects? Would you rather build stuff? Or would you prefer to supervise people? Why is this the type of work you want to do? Why? Why? Why?

- **Who** are you in this dream job? Are you an individual contributor or a team member? Do you consider yourself executive material? Are you a director or manager or supervisor?

- **What** industry is it in? Automotive? Retail? Hospitality? Finance? Technology? What skills, hard and soft, do you need to effectively do this job? What kind of degrees do you need to have? If any? What certifications are mandatory? Or suggested? Does experience trump formal education? Or the other way around? What salary will you receive for this work? If it's a sales position, is commission part of your pay plan? How much will it be? 10%? 50%? 100%?

- **Where** will you do this work physically? Will you work from your home? Will you work remotely? Will you work on a farm? In the suburbs? In a city? Will you commute? Does that commute involve public transportation? Are you working on the factory line? Will you sit at a desk? Are you driving around town? The region? What region? What region of the country will you work in? What country? Will you stay in the country? Will you move to another country? Will you have to travel to faraway locations as part of your responsibilities?

- **When** will you do this dream job? Only during the day? Evenings? Both? Will you work during the nighttime when most people are sleeping? Will you only work on weekdays? How about weekends? What about holidays?

- And finally, **how** will you find this dream job? Will you visit company websites? Will you peruse job boards? Set up alerts to notify you when your dream job is advertised? Will you track social media sites? Will you attend networking events and meetings? And, of course, most importantly, as most career advising professionals will suggest you do—will you seek assistance from your family and friends?

It's a fact that most job seekers land employment because someone they know knows someone they don't know, who usually knows someone who can help make an introduction to a hiring manager. Seek out your connections or create new ones. You never know what will transpire otherwise.

Desire is all well and good but wanting and doing are two different things. I could want to be the best at whatever I want to be. I could wish to do something extraordinary. I could dream of having something I'd never had before. ***But unless I take action, nothing happens.*** And unless there is a drive within me, there won't be action sufficient enough to get me to my goal.

One of the most bantered about mantras in the world of selling is that nothing happens till a sale takes place. Think about that. ***Nothing happens till a sale takes place.*** Regardless of the product or service or outcome desired, nothing happens.

Consider the classic story about the woodsman who enters his cabin in the dead of a winter's night, walks up to the barren and cold fireplace, and says to the fireplace, "Give me heat." What does the fireplace say? "Give me wood."

If you want something, you must do something to get it.

As a job seeker, it's not enough to write down what you want to do. You have to do something to get it. Do a personal assessment to determine your strengths and weaknesses. What do you love, and what do you loathe? What types of activities bring you bliss? What activities are so gut-wrenching and energy-draining that you would rather have root canal surgery WITHOUT Novocaine because THAT would be less painful?

ACTION ITEMS

- If time and money were irrelevant, how would you like to spend your day? Could you be paid for that?
- I learned this from Marcus Buckingham[5]: Take the time to determine what floats your boat and what makes it sink. Recall the things (activities) you've done in your jobs. Or even during your period of transition. What fills you with excitement? What would you do for twenty-nine hours a day? Without the need for a bathroom break? What activity makes time fly? What do you enjoy doing? What activities make you cringe? What about what sucks the oxygen right out of your body? What makes you want to crawl under a rock or into a cave? What activity makes it feel like time is going backward?

---

[5] *Go Put Your Strengths to Work*, Marcus Buckingham.

CHAPTER 6
DRIVEN TO ACHIEVEMENT

Nothing is certain. Anything is possible.
—Eduardo Strauch
1972 Uruguay Air Force
Flight 571 Andes crash survivor

Heading in a general direction is important if you want to grow and improve. But knowing where you're going specifically is so much more critical to your overall success. Writing down the particular requirements of your dream job, the job you would apply to if you saw it described in print or online, sets in motion a series of activities that will get you there sooner. The added bonuses for you are you'll be spending your valued time and money wisely while managing your effort and energy more efficiently and effectively.

IT'S CALLED A GOAL LINE FOR A REASON

As we discussed in the previous chapter, having definiteness of purpose and knowing where you're headed help kick in the drive to gct you where you're going.

Imagine someone tells you they are going to take you and twenty-five of your closest friends on a weeklong trip to a tropical island. All this benevolent, and most mysterious, person asks is that you and your friends meet at the airport in seventy-two hours. Everything will be provided—all travel, rooms, food, spa treatments, even clothing, the works. Everything.

If that offer landed in your lap, do you think you would be able to get your act together, get babysitters lined up, set up bill payments for creditors, rearrange any outstanding appointments for the following week, AND be at the airport check-in counter in three days? Could you? Would you? I know I could. Count on it. Knowing where you're headed is so critical in helping you get there.

Or consider this common scenario in a football game: A quarterback hands off a football to his running back. What does the running back do next? Does he try to avoid being tackled by the opposing team or does he head for the end zone to score a touchdown and collect six points for his team?

Depending upon who you ask, you might get different answers. Since we know the running back gets paid to score touchdowns, you could say he is **driven** to do just that. He is driven with a laser-like beam of focus to move down the field and trained to deal with whatever obstacles he might face along the way. And you know there will be obstacles.

He's driven because on the first day of training camp, the coach gathered the team together and stated his goal for the season was to win the Super Bowl. Not go to the Super Bowl—WIN the Super Bowl! Few people ever remember who lost the Super Bowl but they almost always know who won.

So to that end, every drill that is performed over and over, every play that is designed and practiced, and every meal that is created and consumed is for the sole purpose of hoisting the Vince Lombardi Trophy at the end of the game at the end of the season.

Now, returning to our running back who is only focused on one thing, one outcome, one result—to cross the goal line (*there is a reason why it's called the GOAL line*). If he crosses the goal line enough during the season, he might expect to receive additional cash, performance bonuses, and possibly some lucrative paid product endorsements at year-end.

While he is focused on his goal, the opposing team is focused on him because THEIR goal is to stop him. They will get in his way and make it difficult for him to complete his mission. They will track him down like heat-seeking missiles search and destroy enemy tanks and equipment.

His teammates might be in front of him impeding his forward progress. He might have to run sideways or even away from the target end zone so he can locate and find another way to run down the field and score.

While his hometown fans are cheering him on and supporting his every move, every step, the opposing fans are yelling at him and screaming that his shoelaces are untied or other sentiments that are not appropriate for inclusion in this book. If it's snowing, don't be surprised if a stray snowball or two or multiple snowballs are hurled in his general direction.

It doesn't matter what obstacles he faces, who those

obstacles are, or what they sound like. He is driven to score because his coach established the goal on day one—WIN THE SUPER BOWL!

So make no mistake. As much as he doesn't want to be tackled, he does want to score. Therein lies the glory.

Why am I telling you all this? Unless you establish a specific, directed, and concrete goal for yourself in your job search, you will not be driven to achieve that goal. You will lack the discipline to do what must be done, especially when you don't want to do what must be done to cross your goal line.

And what is your job search goal? It is NOT to get a job. There are plenty of jobs up for grabs regardless of the time of year or state of the job market. ***Your goal is to get YOUR dream job.*** It's what we discussed in the previous chapter. Know where you're heading tomorrow based on your assessment of where you were yesterday and where you are today. Later on we'll address the discipline you need to land your dream job.

ACTION ITEMS

- Read *Psycho-Cybernetics* by Dr. Maxwell Maltz for some fabulous insights about goal setting and achieving those goals.
- Write the job ad you would respond to if you saw it online or in print. Use the six question words from the previous chapter—why, who, what, where, when, and how—in bundles of questions to guide you.
- List some distractions that you will ignore as you settle into your job search. Preparing for what's coming will better prepare you for the job at hand—finding your next job.

CHAPTER 7
IT'S ALL ABOUT THE CUSTOMER

The answer is yes.
What is your question?

When you're in sales, there's no guarantee that if you're nice to your customers they will tell their friends how wonderful you are. No guarantee.

I do, however, guarantee that if you bamboozle them, rip them off, or pull the wool over their eyes, they'll tell everyone that you did so, including your enemies. And they'll remember what you were wearing, whether it was raining or sunny the day you did it, and how poorly you treated them. Until the day they die. Or the day you die. Whichever comes first.

Customers care about themselves more than they care about their salesperson. It's not mean or malicious—it's human nature. I can't fault customers for wanting what they want. Heck, I'm a customer, too, sometimes. I might be interested in helping my salesperson, but my focus is ultimately way more on me and satisfying my needs than it is on satisfying theirs.

Successful salespeople rely on a solid pipeline and book of satisfied customers. It behooves these solution providers to put the spotlight on their customers. If you believe that ideology (and I trust you do), allow me to turn an age-old adage that has been around as long as forever onto its head. This is my philosophy regarding the relationship between customer and salesperson:

> *The customer is NOT always right,*
> *but they are ALWAYS the customer.*

If a salesperson doesn't take care of their customer, rest assured, there is another salesperson lurking, biding their time, and waiting in the wings to swoop in and make the sale.

I LOVE YOU, MOM

In my early training in sales, I learned that managing a customer relationship was analogous to dealing with your mom—assuming you love and respect your mom. Treating your customer with care, respecting their wishes, and addressing their concerns is no different than how you would expect someone to treat your mom. Anything short of that is disrespectful and demonstrates a lack of empathy toward your customer.

Over the years I've come to embrace this dual-edged mindset—the customer is always the customer, and treat them like you would want your mom to be treated. I attribute my success in sales to this attitude. I've been professing to job seekers to consider adopting this belief and way of thinking.

Assume the hiring managers you're reaching out to

and trying to get interviews with are your customers. Assume there are other "salespeople" vying for their attention—in fact, count on it. Most importantly, treat these hiring managers as if they were your mom. Do this and you just might improve your chances of landing your dream job. As I was taught all those years ago, if you find yourself saying things to your customer that you wouldn't want another salesperson to say to your mom, then why are you saying those things? Stop. Immediately. Treat your customers with dignity and respect. If those customers are hiring managers, need I say more?

A KNIGHT IN SHINING ARMOR

When you are preparing for your next interview, try this. Imagine that sometime during your interview the hiring manager stops you in your tracks, possibly midsentence during one of your replies. Just flat out interrupts you and stops you from speaking. She reaches for her phone, calls her administrative assistant, and asks him to cancel the remaining interviews scheduled for the rest of the week because their knight in shining armor (that's YOU!) is sitting across from her. When she hangs up, she looks at you and asks, "Where have you been!? What rock have you been hiding under!? And why has it taken so long for us to meet each other?"

Why wouldn't you imagine that scenario playing out during your interview? You wouldn't go into the interview thinking it's a waste of time and that you are not well suited for the position, right? Right!? What would be so horrible if you envisioned a hiring manager jumping out of their chair and offering you a job in their organization? Before the end of your interview!

On the wide, continuous spectrum of THIS IS TERRIBLE to THIS IS GREAT, what would be the worst thing that could happen? THIS IS TERRIBLE! What would be the best thing that could happen? THIS IS GREAT! Hmmmm, I say, focus on greatness. Why would you choose any other option?

You choose other options because that's what most normal human beings do—they plan for the worst and hope for the best. I'm just as guilty, believe me. Way too many times I've envisioned horrible outcomes. I wasn't surprised when those premonitions became reality. I expected something horrible, and something horrible happened.

However, there have also been times when I expected success and was pleased when those victories transpired. Because I expected those results, I wasn't surprised. You can do that, too. You SHOULD do that, too. Why wouldn't you? Why wouldn't you expect the best possible outcome—landing your dream job?

ACTION ITEMS

- Put the proverbial spotlight on the hiring manager. Remember, it's about them, not you.
- Check your ego at the door. You want the hiring manager to get top billing. The hiring manager's longing to be coddled takes precedence over your desire to be loved. As much as she cares about what you know, she really wants to know you care.
- Plan for the best...and expect it.
- Create a list of possible outcomes that could result from an interview. Rate them on a scale of THIS IS TERRIBLE to THIS IS GREAT.

CHAPTER 8
TIPS FOR THE FIRST-TIME JOB SEEKER

I can't pay the bills yet, 'cause I have no skills yet
The world is a big scary place!
But somehow I can't shake, the feeling I might make
A difference to the human race!
—Princeton in Avenue Q

"Welcome! We're glad you're here!"

"Regardless of your scholastic history, background, pedigree, or social standing, we know you have skills, abilities, and talents that you want to use here so we can be better at what we do."

"We can't wait to hear about the latest and greatest technology tips and techniques you've learned and picked up along your journey that brought you here today."

"I suspect you're chomping at the bit like a thoroughbred racehorse ready to bolt out of the starting gate, even though you're still just a young pony."

EVERY PROFESSIONAL WAS AN AMATEUR

Hopefully, you'll meet hiring managers with these open-minded philosophies. That would be nice, right? How refreshing to meet someone who understands what you're feeling and how much you want to contribute to the workplace.

But alas, in Project Management 101 we are taught to plan for the worst and hope for the best. I believe there is some validity in that mentality—certainly when it comes to your job search and the pool of hiring managers you could meet in potential interviews. You've got to be prepared for the slings and arrows that will be aimed at you.

At a minimum, as you set out on your first search for your dream job, you can expect to hear the following two objections (in no particular order):

- You don't have a college degree, or the right one.
- You don't have any experience.

First, let's address college degrees. College degree requirements might be tough to circumvent in your job search. The Automatic Tracking System (ATS) that most companies use to vet job applicants compares keywords and statements on your resume to the company's job requirements. If certain matches are not made, your resume gets tossed aside and you are no longer in the running. So if a college degree is missing from your resume and a college degree is required, you're out quicker than the time it takes to read this sentence. Yikes!

WHO DO YOU KNOW?

One way you can overcome that cold, heartless, and insensitive system is to have someone who can help bypass the process; having an extensive network of contacts can help you manage the ATS. You might know someone (or know someone who knows someone you do NOT know) who can get you in front of a hiring manager, even if you don't have a degree. How? Your contact can walk your resume up to a hiring manager and hand it directly to them with a personal note of recommendation. Or your friend can send your resume via email combined with a warm introduction. Either way, the company's ATS will be none the wiser nor will it ever get the chance to cast its evil eyes upon your resume!

COLLEGE, SCHMOLLEGE.

Here's my take on college degrees: Some of the dumbest people I know, or know of, have graduated from college. They think because they have a degree that they're smart. They're not. They think that piece of paper implies they're intelligent. Maybe they are. Maybe they're not.

On the other hand, some of the smartest people I know, or know of, don't have a degree or didn't go to college. But they are smart. That's because they know they don't know everything. So they remain curious. They seek guidance and direction. They ask tons of questions. They are lifelong learners.

They, like me, think every time you learn something new that should be your first clue that you aren't as smart as you think you are. Every time something new comes along, you should realize there's so much more you don't know and, therefore, so much more to learn. A lot more. I believe in the following philosophy popularized by Napoleon Hill and summed up nicely by the Dalai Lama: "Whenever I speak, I share what I know. But when I listen, who knows what I'll learn."

If it's a college degree you're lacking, no problem. Tap into your network because someone out there can provide you with the opportunity to discuss and demonstrate your smarts and initiative. But you have to dig into your past and collect those moments to prove your know-how.

OTHER TYPES OF EXPERIENCE

This brings us to the other objection you can expect to deal with on your quest to land your dream job. If a hiring manager questions your experience or lack thereof, that's your cue to discuss any paid employment you've had. Or you can talk about your volunteering efforts and community involvement—if you've done that type of service. If you lack volunteer experience and community service, then go get some.

Regardless of whether you got paid or not, here's where you'll elaborate on your SATs. Describe what problems you solved over the years, expand upon the actions you took to solve those problems, and proudly state the results you achieved to improve or enhance whatever the situation was before you got involved to make things so much better now.

Brag about the winter storms you trudged through as you shoveled snow in your neighborhood. Better yet, share your process for reaching out to households in other neighborhoods to develop an extended list of clients for snow shoveling services BEFORE the winter storms arrived.

Consider talking about clubs and associations you belonged to and any responsibilities you might have had in them. Times when you lent a hand. Occasions when you led a project or a group of people. Or both.

If they say we're looking for someone who can lead a team, then tell them about situations in which you did just that. If you have led a team, you probably have been required to do things such as negotiate, motivate, delegate, influence, manage, direct, persuade, and supervise. If you haven't led a team, now would be a good time to step up and find a team to lead—or create one and lead it.

If you've done something with a special flair, grace, or technique that hasn't been done before, then you are a trailblazer. Bring that persona and attitude into an interview and watch a hiring manager's attention pique, back straighten, and eyes light up.

Enlist those you know and who know you for assistance in creating this collection of accomplishments and achievements. It's a great way to continue growing your network.

Don't neglect this important step. Also, please ask others to help you capture and catalog your strengths. You'll be amazed at how your network can help you with this valuable aspect of your job search. But only if you have a network of contacts to pull from. So go get help. You deserve it. You won't regret it.

And who knows, in the process of doing all this fact-finding, someone might introduce you to a hiring manager you should meet, mention a company you should investigate, or inform you of a job to which you should apply. Maybe. Maybe not. There's no guarantee that any of that will happen if you do any of those things. No guarantee. I guarantee if you don't, they probably won't. Just saying.

As an aside, I've learned you might not get recognized for winning a deal or getting a job offer on your own. Good for you. The winning, that is. Not getting recognized is not so nice. However, please, please, please do NOT ever lose by yourself. Please!

If you need help, make a phone call, write an email, text, knock on a door, and request assistance. Please get help! That loss might have been prevented if you sought out people around you who would have gladly helped if only you had asked.

Here's an added bonus for doing those activities, all of them—you'll get to check off multiple items on your to-do list, namely:

- Learn new skills (*helpful in your job search*)
- Develop your network (*just as valuable as the skills you'll learn*)
- Work with people from different backgrounds (*help you develop your network*)

Do you see how everything you do is interrelated to everything you do? It is so vital that you get out there and learn, develop, collaborate, and garner the SATs that will differentiate you from your competition.

ACTION ITEMS

- Build your network. It can include friends, family, neighbors, members of the clergy, teachers, professors, ex-bosses, colleagues, and people from whom you buy products and services.
- List activities you've had that capture the essence of who you are.
- Identify problems, obstacles, and hassles you've solved, whether you were paid or not.
- Identify actions you took to solve those problems.
- Highlight the results you achieved to solve those problems. Be specific, think in terms of time saved, money saved, revenues generated, people managed, and effort reduced or simplified.

CHAPTER 9
WHEN YOU HAVE BEEN OUT OF WORK

Keeping my mind on a better life
When happiness is only a heartbeat away
Paradise, can it be all I heard it was
I close my eyes and maybe I'm already there
—Styx

Nobody said what you did yesterday is what you have to do tomorrow. Actually, somebody probably did, but it doesn't mean you have to listen to them. Remember when your parents asked if you'd follow in your friends' footsteps if they did something foolish?

TO THINE OWN SELF BE TRUE

As an unemployed individual, you now have the time to assess where you've been, where you are, and where you want to go. You may even consider that you have an advantage over people who are currently working because they have to go "make the doughnuts." You, on the other hand, can take the time to assess your skills, abilities, and talents. Your SATs.

You also have the time to explore the many different options available to you and where you can use those ***skills, abilities, and talents*** that make you unique, distinguished, and valuable to others.

When you've been out of work for an extended period, it's on you to stay current and involved with the world around you. And as much as I discourage job seekers from watching and listening to all the negative news and energy-depleting, gut-wrenching stories that are paraded in front of our eyes and ears every day, you do need to have an inkling about what's going on in the world. Emphasis on inkling. Be familiar with some international goings-on, be up to date on selected national stories, and be knowledgeable about the people and events that are making the local news nearby and in your immediate region.

Being current is half the battle when you've been out of work for weeks or months or longer. Staying positive and upbeat is critical if you want to be successful in landing your next job.

Regardless of the circumstances surrounding your unemployment, you have to keep your chin up, chest out, and shoulders back. Walking around with your tail between your legs and your chin on your chest is a formula for disaster. It's also two clues you're giving to those in your world that you're downtrodden and depressed—not necessarily in that order.

AGEISM

The older I get, the younger I was, the faster I ran, the harder I hit, and the higher I jumped.
—T-shirt worn by a seventy-year-old recreational volleyball player

Imagine this: A hiring manager is reading your resume and notices that your year of college graduation is missing. Huh? Did you forget to include it? Or did you decide to omit it on purpose because you:

- Are concerned they'll use math to discern your age?
- Don't want to be eliminated from the competition before the race has started?
- Know they can't discriminate against you because of your age?

If you truly believe that last one, then I don't know where you're from, but it must be a beautiful place.

In my humble opinion, I believe if someone is reading your resume and they don't see your college graduation year, they might think you don't want them to know your age. Once that seed is planted in their head, then they might think you are older than most. They might also wonder why you didn't include that important piece of information. Therefore, the one thing you didn't want to draw attention to—your age—is now on stage front and center, commanding the reader's attention. Oops! So much for not making your age part of the equation. Oh well.

I don't believe that's the worst of it, though. I think

what can be more damaging to your candidacy and your efforts to land your next job are these thoughts that can begin to swirl in the hiring manager's head instead: "What else is missing from this resume? What else is this applicant hiding?"

Now, not only are they thinking about your age, but you have them questioning your background, experience, and possibly your character. Worse yet, they might be wondering about your standing as a law-abiding citizen. Ugh!!

I know that's not your intent, but planting seeds of doubt and uncertainty could knock you out of the competition. Maybe. Maybe not. I say, why go there?

If they like you and continue to pursue you, then they'll do a background check and discover what you're omitting after all. If they don't like you, then any college graduation year you include won't help you.

In the end, I'm still not sure if your year of graduation is important to your hiring manager. Maybe it is. Maybe it isn't. I say include it, and see where the chips fall. Keep them focused on you and your character. Do not give them a reason to question or doubt you.

Now, not wanting to be accused of being closed-minded, I believe the scenario described above also holds true for younger job seekers, those individuals who are relatively new to the job market or may not even have gone to college. If that describes you, then you, too, have legitimate concerns your age can be used against you as well.

I'm with you. And again, I believe that deliberately excluding dates that could be used to reverse engineer your age will only raise a hiring manager's curiosity and get them thinking about your age—the one thing you didn't want them doing! IMHO, include important dates.

See what I did there? If you include acronyms such as IMHO in your cover letter, resume, or LinkedIn profile, yet exclude dates, the reader might surmise you also know the meaning of FOMO, ICYMI, and TTYL, you possibly use them regularly throughout your day, and you probably don't have a lot of work experience. Just saying.

OPERATOR, WOULD YOU HELP ME PLACE THIS CALL?

Putting that discussion to rest, here's something else to consider regarding your desire to cover up your age. If your reader is slightly savvy and attuned to things such as age and ageism, you might be unknowingly showing your hand even as you try to hide your age. How?

If you write your phone number this way:

(212) 555-1212

then you probably know what a Walkman is. You probably had one, too. You probably remember when thermal paper was used in a fax machine. Remember when those pages would curl up on the floor? You even know what a fax machine is and what it's used for.

You remember when cable and television were never used in the same sentence. You remember receiving CDs from AOL and Prodigy offering free introductory sign-ups every day. In the mail! EVERY DAY!!

See where I'm going with this? If you place parentheses around the area code of a phone number, then you might as well include your college graduation date because you remember when microwave ovens were things you only saw on *The Jetsons*. You remember watching cartoons on Saturday mornings because that was the ONLY time cartoons were broadcast on television.

Now, a lot of people today write phone numbers with periods like this:

212.555.1212

Looks like an IP address used in computing, right? Hip. Cool. Progressive. Or they might write it like this instead:

212-555-1212

Dashes are totally acceptable. Not as youthful-looking as periods, but still current and up to date.

Do you write phone numbers like this?

(212) MH8-1212

Then I admire your longevity on this planet and will want to sit with you to learn more about your wonderful life.

Seriously, though, when it comes to fighting ageism—and it is a fight—I suggest you consider periods or dashes when writing out your phone number. Save parentheses for when you want to include additional information in a sentence. Enough said.

ACTION ITEMS

- Review your resume and include pertinent dates. You don't want your reader to guess when you graduated from college or what years you worked at what companies.
- Check out Roadtrip Nation. On their website you'll find the following description of this longtime running television series: We take road trips to capture empowering stories that give you the confidence and tools to find a career that matters to us. If you're looking for direction about what you want to do or validation that you are doing the right thing, then visit Roadtrip Nation and prepare to be inspired to pursue what you want to do.

CHAPTER 10
THE OLDER WORKER

When I get older losing my hair, many years from now.
—John Lennon and Paul McCartney

Let's continue our discussion and address the elephant in the room, shall we? Ageism. There are now four generations in society working or seeking employment. At the same time! That's a lot of employees and applicants in the employment pool. Is it any wonder that there is bumping and banging and contention in the crowded waters?

WHY CAN'T WE ALL JUST GET ALONG?

Older and mature people are being forced to supplement their income reserves. This older generation is taking on roles and positions that were normally reserved for high school and college students. Career plans have been uprooted and tossed to the winds because of unforeseen layoffs and downsizings. Retirement plans that were created and tweaked over the years have been put on hold.

Meanwhile, the younger generation is looking to start building their fortunes and stockpiling funds for future plans yet to be actualized. However, *those* plans are being squashed and/or put on hold because jobs they normally would be working at are being taken over by older workers.

Younger people are asking the older folks to step aside. They're saying, "You had your chance to work and amass fortunes, now it's our turn. We want to start our lives as well as create a circle of friends and family and colleagues. We want what you always talked about and what we saw growing up minus the layoffs and vanishing pensions."

We also know that Millennials and Gen Zers want less stress even as they seek growth-oriented careers. Good for them. Why not?

It is frustrating for everyone and frightening as well. Older folk used to brag about job security and stability. Thirty years of steadily increasing responsibilities at this company, forty years of guaranteed employment at that company. A gold watch here, lifetime health benefits over there. Those scenarios are slowly becoming memories and things that grandparents now reminisce about with their children and grandchildren.

In 1950 a company would invite your dad to fly across the country to visit an office and interview for a position. If things looked positive, then your mom would be flown out to preview neighborhoods with the CEO's wife. At night all four would have dinner together. Then your dad and mom would return home, the necessary papers would be signed, and the entire family would uproot itself, move to the new location, set up new roots, and stay put for decades. Not anymore. Now you can read about that mystical world in Wikipedia and the history books.

Older job applicants are hearing objections such as:

- You're overqualified. No, wait! You're way over-qualified!
- Your salary and benefit requirements are too high.
- We're concerned you're taking this job as a filler or gap position until your ideal job comes along so you can make more money.

That last one drives me crazy because we all know thirty-year-olds who have had three jobs since graduating from college. Three jobs in seven years! And each new job comes with a pay increase AND signing bonus! What the hey? Just saying.

I'm pretty sure when Captain "Sully" Sullenberger landed his aircraft in the Hudson River there wasn't a passenger on that plane praying that their pilot was thirty years old. I suspect there's no way a thirty-year-old pilot could have been prepared for that situation. I'm not saying that a thirty-year-old could not have replicated what Sully did, but a thirty-year-old pilot couldn't have been on this planet long enough to put in the cockpit hours that Captain Sully had. It's just not possible.

Said thirty-year-old pilot could've been a newlywed or a new parent, looking forward to a long and happy life. This young pilot could've easily panicked, and the outcome would've been a lot worse. Possibly fatal.

Captain Sully, a sixty-plus-year-old pilot, already had

grown children and grandchildren. He was cool, calm, and collected on that plane on that day. He had lived a fuller life compared to a younger, less experienced pilot still wet behind the ears.

Luckily, for the passengers and crew, Captain Sully was the right man sitting in the right place at the right time during the right set of circumstances. He was even trained as a glider pilot, which was an added bonus as the events of that fateful day unfolded. Sully was probably thinking, "I can do this. I've trained for this. I wasn't planning on this, but I can do this," as history has shown he did.

Now I'm not saying that handling an airborne commercial airliner that does not have any working engines in air space situated over the most populated area in the northeastern United States in January in near-freezing temperatures is comparable to landing your next job (pun intended), but don't you see that, given your SATs, you could be the right person sitting in the right place at the right time during the right set of circumstances. You can't control the circumstances, but you can control your reactions to those circumstances.

I know. It's not fair to have to jump through hoops to show your worth. You shouldn't have to place your value in a showcase in hopes that a customer will buy it. Life is not fair. You know that; otherwise, you wouldn't be reading this. Even though it's not definitive proof, pull out your birth certificate and look for the phrase "Life is fair." Let me save you time and effort—it's not there. Anywhere. Not even on the back. Life is not fair.

Lucky for you with age comes wisdom. You're comfortable with the knowledge that tomatoes are fruit but wise enough to not include them in a fruit salad.

Use your wisdom. Recall your past successes. Pull out the life experiences that make you unique and bring them to the stage. Tout your grace under fire.

Ageism is real. Strap yourself in and sell yourself. Demonstrate to hiring managers that you've encountered scenarios similar to the ones they're facing today. Share stories about problems you successfully managed because of storms that you've weathered. Highlight roadblocks you've overcome. "Been there, done that" are words you can say proudly and confidently. Shout them from the rooftops for all to hear.

While we're at it, allow me to remain on my pedestal and continue my diatribe. You know that we don't slow down because we get old. We get old because we slow down. Colonel Sanders started Kentucky Fried Chicken when he was sixty-five years young. Grandma Moses started painting when she was eighty years of age.

Get thee moving! Bring your SATs to bear. The world needs them, and you're just the right guy or gal to show us what you have. We're counting on you!

ACTION ITEMS

- Read about Colonel Sanders and Grandma Moses. While you're at it, check out Julia Child, Ray Kroc, and Bernie Marcus. Take direction from these successful senior citizens who achieved their success after others like them who believe that age is just a number. If you want to hang up your hat, retire, or go out to graze in the pasture, more power to you. I suspect, if you picked up this book, that might not be you—even more power to you.

- List your SATs.

- Figure out how your SATs distinguish you from other humans on this planet so you can articulate those differences to additional human beings.

- Practice answering this question, "Why does someone with your experience want this job?"

- Then practice answering this question, "Why would someone want to hire you?"

CHAPTER 11
PRESENTING YOURSELF PROFESSIONALLY

*Customers may not remember you were five minutes
early. They will never forget you were five seconds late.
Get there early.*

—*Joey Himelfarb*

Humans communicate in several ways with one another. When it comes to selling yourself, one of three communication modes usually takes center stage. First, the words we use in conversation. The actual words we choose to use can help or hurt our sales pitch. Know who you are talking to, and adjust your approach accordingly.

Second, how we use the words we choose in conversation can help or hinder our message. Our tone, pace, inflections, volume, pauses, and emotions affect our audience of one or many. For example, the way we speak to a five-year-old is slightly different from the way we speak to a twenty-five-year-old (*depending upon the twenty-five-year-old, of course!*).

Finally, most of our communication with each other is nonverbal. Sometimes what we don't say speaks volumes and can easily and innocently derail the message we are conveying, and we don't even realize we are our own worst enemy.

Countless books have been written about nonverbal communication. Google it to see for yourself. For our purposes here, I would like to share a few ways we communicate with each other without saying a word.

WHAT YOU DON'T SAY SPEAKS VOLUMES

Imagine you are sitting across from a hiring manager, and they have their hands clasped or their arms or legs are crossed. Those are the first clues that you are not connecting with them. They are closed off to you and may not be listening to you or even paying attention to you. Your job is to get that person to unclench their hands or uncross their arms or legs and open up to you.

What if your hands are clasped or your arms or legs are crossed? They might think they're not connecting with you. They might be turned off by your closeness and resign them-selves to believing you're not the right candidate. Maybe. Maybe not.

If the person interviewing you plays with their hair, covers their mouth, or touches their face when they talk or demonstrates some other kind of nervous tick or twitch, they could be withholding information or misleading you—or just be nervous. Because this is what you see and not what they're saying, you might be inclined to be taken aback or possibly turned off. Either way, any of these feelings could affect how you perform in this interview. Maybe. Maybe not.

Conversely, if you're the one exhibiting these slight body

language movements, you could be turning off the interviewer and unknowingly ruin your chances to move through the process. Maybe. Maybe not.

What if the person you're meeting with doesn't look you in the eyes? I'm not suggesting they stare at you unblinkingly. I'm talking about making eye contact as they share information about themselves, their company, or the job at hand. I'm talking about making a connection on a human level. If they don't do that, then you might have reason to doubt their integrity. They might be telling you the truth and being open with you, but this nonverbal action is your subconscious cue to doubt their honesty. Some people just have a hard time with eye contact, which might be why they're not looking at you. And that could throw you for a loop during your conversation. Maybe. Maybe not.

What if you don't make eye contact with them? Imagine what they're thinking if your eyes don't meet theirs as you share stories and experiences from your past or describe how you would help them in the future. I don't believe they would be as forgiving with you as you might be with them. They might be. Maybe not. I'm suggesting you don't want to plant that seed of uncertainty in their head. Just saying.

This eye contact issue can be challenging when you're face to face with a hiring manager. The challenge can become exasperating if your interview is virtual. Regardless of the application used for your video interview, it is imperative that you look into your camera lens when talking to a hiring manager.

DOES ANYONE REALLY KNOW WHAT TIME IT IS?

For me, the most serious nonverbal action you should never, ever do during an interview is something most of us do most of the time, without giving it a moment's thought. It's so innocuous, so simple, so unthought of in the course of our days. We even wonder why it's such a big deal. And yet, it could be so devastating that whatever good was created before you did it would become null and void and completely negated. Worse still, it would probably be remembered for a long time, if not forever.

Imagine you're sitting in your interview, and the interviewer nonchalantly glances at her Apple Watch. Ugh!! What are you thinking? She's bored. She's not interested in what I have to say or share. We're not connecting. She might be thinking about how much longer your answer is going to be to the question she asked. She might be thinking about ending the interview. She might be thinking this is the worst use of her time. She would rather be somewhere else. She wishes this would end. Right now.

In fact, she just might be curious what time it is. She might be trying to ensure she has enough time to ask all she wants to ask of you. She might want to ensure she leaves you enough time to ask your questions as well. Maybe. Maybe not.

Now what if you nonchalantly look at your wristwatch? What is she thinking? You're bored. You're not interested in what she has to say or share. We're not connecting. She might be thinking about ending the interview. She might be thinking you are thinking this is the worst use of your time. She is thinking you would rather be somewhere else and that you are wishing this interview would end. Right now. Maybe. Maybe not. Unfortunately, what the interviewer might be thinking is: We are so done with this candidacy! Don't glance at your watch!

As you are sitting down to begin your interview, ask if it would be ok to have a pen and pad of paper in front of you so you may take notes during the conversation. I have never heard of any interviewer who did NOT allow notes to be taken during an interview. Please let me know if you ever meet such a person.

Sometime during your interview you might notice the person you're speaking with lean forward after you say something of importance or value. At that moment, and as discreetly as possible, jot down a word or two that will help you remember what you just said that got that individual to open up and lean in.

Why is that important? Because when you write your follow-up thank you note—you ALWAYS write a follow-up thank you note—you will refer to that comment in the note. By doing so you will subconsciously alert the individual to what you said in your conversation. And in doing so, you will differentiate yourself from your competition and rise above the crowded field of applicants.

Another thing to consider if you're fortunate enough to be invited for an in-person interview is to look the part— look like you belong. Don't go to an accounting job dressed as a lumberjack. Don't go to a hardware store interview in a three-piece suit. Wear the uniform of the team.

Let me share this story from a job seeker I met at one of my seminars years ago. Donna (not her real name) was researching a company for an upcoming interview. As she was perusing the company's website, she couldn't help but notice that prominently displayed and emblazoned on every page were the company's logo and colors.

"Prominently displayed and emblazoned" were not her exact words, but she definitely noticed the company's colors everywhere on every page. Her eyes lit up as she described her experience and the idea that popped into her head because of this observation.

She submitted a cover letter and resume for the position. She was invited in for an interview and eventually was offered employment at this firm. It was only after she accepted their offer and reported for work did she inquire as to why they hired her. "In addition to your background and experience, we couldn't help but notice how you looked like you belong here," the hiring manager said.

Why did Donna look like she belonged there? When Donna went on her interview, she purposely and strategically wore the colors of the company that were prominently displayed on the website.

Subtle. Creative. Out of the box thinking. YOU GO, GIRL!

ACTION ITEMS

- Go to YouTube and search for "nonverbal communication." See for yourself how sometimes the things we don't say speak volumes.
- Roleplay an interview. Have someone act as the hiring manager and let them ask you questions you think you might be asked in your interview. Pretend you are the interviewee. Wait! You ARE the interviewee! Duh!
- Record your roleplay using audio and video, and then review your performance. Listen to your answers. Remember good ones that you can use in actual interviews. Rephrase the not-so-good ones so they'll sound better in your interviews. Eliminate answers you don't like or don't sound quite right.
- Look for nonverbal communication in the video recording: folded arms, hands clenched together with fingers entwined, legs crossed, eye contact or lack thereof, staring at the ceiling, checking your wristwatch, and fidgeting with your pen or notebook. You did ask the hiring manager if you could take notes with your pen and notebook, right?

- Write the words "LOOK HERE!" in boldface on a small sign. Tape the sign next to your computer's camera lens. As an added reminder for you to look directly into the camera lens during your interview, draw an arrow pointing to the lens. The person you're talking to will be grateful for your attention to this detail; way too many people overlook this in virtual conversations. Then add another feather to your cap for separating yourself from your competition!

CHAPTER 12
CAN-DO ATTITUDE

Failure will not overtake me if my desire
for success is strong.

—Og Mandino

I used to work for AT&T Submarine Systems, Inc. SSI was responsible for the design, manufacturing, installation, and maintenance of transoceanic fiber optic communications cables. Some of my responsibilities were assisting with cable manufacturing, supervising the loading of cable systems onto cable ships, and installing these cables around the world.

On a few occasions I had the opportunity to swap my physics and mechanical engineering hats for a sales hat. I was asked by our sales team to present, in layman's terms, the scientific concepts and processes that made it possible for connecting landmasses via undersea fiber optic communications cables. When I would finish my presentations, the sales team would thank me and send me back to the field. The sales team would then sell these multimillion-dollar systems and be handsomely rewarded for their efforts.

I very much enjoyed being on stage and leading conversations about these technologies and asked if I could join the sales team. Unfortunately, there weren't any openings. So I looked outside the company to embark on a drastic career change. I ended up getting an interview for a sales support position at Hewlett-Packard (HP), supporting the global account team that called on AT&T.

After the interview I followed up with the proverbial thank you note and then, three days later, the follow-up phone call. The hiring manager told me that even though they liked me, the company imposed a hiring freeze. To which I said, "Ok. May I call you next month to see if anything changes?" I was told I could so I did. The hiring manager wasn't in when I called so I left a message saying I was checking in and was still interested.

No response back from the hiring manager so I called again in a few weeks. Again, he wasn't in so I left a similar message as before. No response for several weeks so I called again but this time I left a slightly longer voicemail message. "It's not my intent to hound or stalk you. You said I could follow up so I am because I liked what I heard during my interview and believe I would be a valuable addition to your team. If you want me to cease and desist, then I will stop calling you. Otherwise, I would love to talk to you more about this position."

Still no response.

I called on the fifteenth of every ensuing month. If he answered, he would tell me the freeze was still on. I would then express my continued interest in the company and position on his team. This exchange carried on for about a year. Finally, imagine my delight when the manager called to let me know the hiring freeze was lifted, they were down to four candidates vying for two slots, and would I consider coming in to continue the process.

After returning to continue the interview process, I was offered a sales support position responsible for assisting the account managers across all the business units of AT&T. It was my entree into the world of sales. I was to work with customers to help them with anything regarding HP.

I was told that my work experience at ATT-SSI was important to the decision to hire me. Knowing how AT&T employees worked with vendors would prove valuable to my success. But it was my polite persistence and professional, relentless pursuit of asking for the opportunity to join the sales team that gave me the edge.

By not taking no as an answer, let alone no response, I demonstrated the kind of dogged determination that a salesperson must possess and that HP valued.

I was to support our sales team for eighteen months so I helped fulfill equipment orders. I answered questions about computer configurations. I coordinated appointments and sales presentations. I enlisted assistance from subject matter experts when I didn't have the answers needed to satisfy our customers' needs. All these activities helped me learn about HP's products and services as well as become better equipped to work with customers.

As luck would have it, one of our account managers retired, and I was promoted into his role thirteen months ahead of schedule.

I've never looked back. I enjoyed my new professional life and thrived in the challenge of serving my clients.

POSITIVE AFFIRMATIONS

The jury is out about whether positive affirmations are all they're cracked up to be. I think they work, but that's me. Others feel differently, and that's ok.

Positive affirmations are simple, positive, and present-based messages you repeat to yourself on a regular schedule or on an as-needed basis. You state you are someone, you do some action, or you have something that you strive to be, do, or have.

It's positive because, well, positive beats negative every day. It's simple because life's complicated enough as it is. And it's present-based because the object of stating these positive affirmations is to get you to act AS IF you are, do, or have what you want. Acting as if is critical to your success because it sets your brain in motion to behave in such a way that you're where you want to be even though you're not.

If you want your next job, saying you WILL have it sends a signal to your brain that you lack a job. That's negative and brings you down. Saying you HAVE the job you want and acting as if you ARE employed tricks your brain into thinking you're in a position of abundance. That's positive and uplifting.

This is all brought to bear because science teaches us that your mind sometimes cannot distinguish between what is real and what is imaginary. *Psychology Today* states that research shows mental pictures are almost as effective as true physical practice and that doing both is more effective than either alone. That is important because when you believe in something that doesn't exist or you act as if it does, your mind cannot recognize the discrepancy. Therefore, it will seek out ways and means to help you be there, get there, and stay there. If your faith falters, then it will take longer to get to and maintain that state.

Read that paragraph again. It might be one of the most important ones in this book. Most successful individuals understand that notion and have adopted that philosophy to help them achieve great things. It can also help you stay the course and keep you focused on getting the job you want.

Here are some sample positive affirmations to help you be, do, or have.

- I am healthy.
- I am wise.
- I am confident.
- I have the skills to perform the job at hand.
- I am financially independent.
- I am grateful for all that I have.
- I write compelling cover letters.
- I am empathetic and understanding.
- I am positive and upbeat.
- I have healthy relationships.
- I am in control of my attitude and emotions.
- I am the best.

ACTION ITEMS

- Look up "positive affirmations" in your favorite search engine and create your own list of daily positive affirmations.
- Write down some of your favorite affirmations on index cards or Post-It Notes and stick these on walls and mirrors to remind you about who you are, what you want to do, and what you want to have.
- Say these positive affirmations out loud. You want your brain to adopt them as if they were real.

CHAPTER 13
POSITIVE BEATS NEGATIVE EVERY DAY

The sun will come out tomorrow.

—Annie

One morning I went outside to retrieve the newspaper. When I sat down at my kitchen table, I opened the sports section. I always read the sports section first because I want to read about winners. I want to read about what they did to win. I want to learn about the fits and starts that got them to the winner's circle, platform, or pedestal.

To my surprise, emblazoned across the first page, front and center, I read the leading story headline, "Josh Himelfarb. Hillsborough Senior Is the Courier News Volleyball Player of the Year." Accompanying the headline was a photo of my smiling and confident seventeen-year-old athlete son.

Wow! Proud dad indeed!

Obviously, Josh knew about this because he was interviewed and photographed beforehand but never told me about this award. When I saw Josh later that day and asked him about the article, he shrugged it off. And when I asked him how he achieved that accolade, he couldn't explain it. Maybe so. But I could.

Josh and his brother participated in many competitive sports growing up: baseball, basketball, football, soccer, swimming, volleyball. Before every game, match, or event, I would send them a text that I had saved on my phone. In my messaging app, I would type "kp," press return, and the following message would appear for immediate delivery to their cell phones:

> Keep repeating to yourself:
> I AM THE BEST. I AM THE BEST.
> And one day you will be.

They'd receive the text and respond back with, "Enough with the stupid text, Dad." So I would send it one more time for good measure. Why not? Wouldn't you? Couldn't hurt, right!?

Now I'm not saying that repeatedly sending that text to Josh earned him the distinction of being the Volleyball Player of the Year. I could have told him he wasn't the strongest kid on the team because he wasn't. I could have told him he didn't jump the highest because he didn't. I could have told him he wasn't the tallest kid on the squad because he definitely was not. I could have told him he didn't hit the ball harder than anyone else because he did not.

I could have told him all these things. I most definitely could have. Instead, I planted in his head that he should consider himself the best and that one day he will be. And voila!

BLAH! BLAH! BLAH!

We know that the person we talk to the most throughout the day is ourself. And we know the majority of things we say or think to ourselves are negative or lean toward the negative end of the positive-negative spectrum.

What are you telling yourself? Are you tearing yourself down? Are you walking around with your tail between your legs, shoulders slumped, chin on your chest? Are you the president of the Pity Party? Or are you building yourself up? Is your head held high, shoulders back, chest out? Do you exude confidence?

Scientists tell us that thinking positively conditions our mind into paying attention to our surroundings and noticing things that will help us. The irony is that those things are always out there; we just don't see them because our negative tendencies dominate our psyche and impair our vision.

I suggest that steering your thoughts toward the positive can help you better deal with the stuff the world throws at you. I won't guarantee that these positive thoughts and ideas will generate positive outcomes. I can't. But I do believe that thinking negatively probably will not get you what you want or desire. Just saying.

LIMITING BELIEFS

Inaction breeds doubt and fear. Action breeds confidence and courage. If you want to conquer the negative elements in your life, don't sit at home and think about it. Go out and get busy!

—*Dale Carnegie*

Imagine sitting at a table with another individual. They are consumed with self-limiting beliefs that hold them back from trying anything new. They are fearful of failure, rejection, pain, hurt, embarrassment, and all those things that stop us in our tracks. Heck, in their mind they believe every solution has a problem.[6] Consequently, they can't conceive of creating something spectacular or wonderful, let alone achieving anything glorious or momentous.

At the same time they look across at you and can't help but think you have the Midas touch. They believe everything you touch turns to gold and whatever you do exceeds everyone's expectations. In their mind you can leap tall buildings in a single bound and stop a speeding locomotive with your bare hands. You cannot do anything wrong. You are godlike, bordering on immortal. Yikes!

Now while she's beating herself up and admiring you, you are cursing the ground you walk on and questioning your worth and value. You can't believe how unaccomplished you are and what a disgrace you are to your friends and family. In Wikipedia, alongside the entry for "Imposter Syndrome," is a picture of you. And while you're painting

---

[6] Credit to Albert Einstein for suggesting we minimize our contact with negative people—they have a problem for every solution.

a horrible picture of yourself, you think the other person is God's gift to the world and can do anything under the sun. In fact, you think they ARE the sun. Sheesh!

If the two of you are left alone to your own devices, how will either of you accomplish anything!? You're both languishing in your personal pity parties and waiting for the other person to do something earth-shattering. Well, there's only one way the earth will shake—one of you has to take the bull by the horns, talk yourself out of the negative spiral you're allowing to engulf you, and take over. Get off your duff and make something happen.

You see, there are three types of people on this planet. The first type makes things happen. The second type watches what happens. And the third type asks, "What just happened?"

Think of a concert or a play: The musicians or actors are on stage—the first type. Members of the audience are the second type. The people outside the arena are hearing thunderous applause—the third type.

My son Jared is the first type. For as long as I can remember, he has never been the quiet one—in any room. Starting in the maternity ward, he did what was necessary to attract attention. His incessant screaming, in retrospect, might not have been colic—it probably was his yearning to be seen and heard. And boy, has he fulfilled that desire. Fast- forward thirty-one years: As the lead singer of two different music groups, he is the epitome of the person on stage who makes stuff happen.

If you're looking for a job, you don't need to scream, cry, sing, or play guitar. You do need to make stuff happen, though. You need to get off the fence, your couch, first base, or any other metaphor, real or imagined, that gets you from where you are to where you want to be. Once again, there is no guarantee if you take any of these actions that you will be successful. I guarantee if you don't, you probably won't. Just saying.

ACTION ITEMS

- Squelch any limiting beliefs you have that are stymying your progress. You need to strut your stuff, get on your soapbox, and extol the virtues of your SATs. To paraphrase world-renowned Olympic gymnastic coach Béla Károlyi: "You can do it!"
- You need to speak to yourself in a positive way. Read *What You Say When You Talk to Your Self* by Dr. Shad Helmstetter. You'll be glad you did.

CHAPTER 14
DON'T PAINT YOUR KITCHEN

Everything in moderation...including moderation.
—*Oscar Wilde*

Discipline, loosely defined and depending upon who you ask, is doing what needs to get done, even when you don't want to do it.

Let me illustrate with the following example: Assume that this book is striking a chord with you so that first thing tomorrow morning you are going to march into your kitchen, make a pot of coffee or your drink of choice, open your laptop, and begin your job search in earnest. But alas, when you sit down at your kitchen table, you're not truly focused because you're not sure where to start or what to do.

Actually, you do because you're reading this book. But you're only human. I get that so one of two scenarios play out in your mind. Either you don't want to get out of your comfort zone because you're looking for something to do that's pleasant, not painful, and easy, not challenging. Or there are things you just don't want to do for various reasons: lack of knowledge coupled with doubt and uncertainty about how to do certain things, fear of failure in trying things never attempted before, or degrees of difficulty, to name a few.

So while your procrastination intensifies and you wallow in indecision, you can't help but notice how drab the room looks. "Maybe I'll paint the kitchen," you say to yourself. Because even though you have to prep the room and move the fridge away from the wall, painting your kitchen is relatively easy to do. Remove anything hanging on the walls, spackle remnant holes, apply painter's tape wherever necessary to protect cabinet and appliance surfaces, and lay down a drop cloth to protect the floor. Assemble the necessary supplies and materials, and off you go. The whole job shouldn't take more than a day. Easy peasy, right?

Here's the problem, actually, several problems, with this scenario:

1. You're not performing your job search.
2. Other job seekers, vying for the job YOU want, are doing the work to get the interview that helps them land the job YOU want. And one of these proactive, disciplined job seekers WILL land the job YOU want. Count on it.
3. You're not in the game.
4. Did I mention you're not performing your job search?

Now here's the kicker. Your newly painted kitchen has you revved up and excited about getting your nose back to the grindstone so you can resume your job search tomorrow. But the next day when you sit down in your newly painted, bright, and radiant kitchen, you nonchalantly glance through the door into the adjoining dining room. Your drab, old, weathered-looking, and beat-up dining room. Uh oh! Guess what happens next?

Yep. Time to paint the dining room. Time to recreate that feeling that comes from doing something fun and enjoyable while being comfortable and carefree. This time, however, there are several large pieces of furniture to move. There are wall chair rails, ceiling crown moldings, and a fragile, delicate hanging chandelier to contend with. This job will take two days to complete. Maybe three.

Things only get worse from here. Because now that these two rooms are freshly painted and given a new lease on life, you decide to paint the entire house. All of it. How could you not? The bathrooms. The laundry room. The hallways. And don't forget the entrance foyer with its vaulted ceilings, skylights, and decorative lighting sconces.

Six to eight weeks pass by if you're lucky, and you haven't done anything to further your cause. But boy, your house sure looks good! May I suggest the following: ***DON'T PAINT YOUR KITCHEN!***

Knuckle down. Do what you have to do to land your next job. Get paid. THEN hire a painter. They are definitely better at it than you and can probably do it quicker with less effort and more efficiency. Let them earn their keep. They deserve it. Besides, they could definitely use the money.

So if you buy into that ideology and refocus on your job search, there are certain activities you have to do to land your next job. For example, you have to:

- **Perform** a self-assessment about your values, your skillset, your strengths and weaknesses, the things that rock your world, and those that shake the foundation under your feet.
- **Research** the companies that you have targeted by going to their websites, reading their 10-K reports if they are public companies, and googling them.
- **Reach** out to your network to see if there's anybody you know who may know somebody that works at your targeted companies.
- **Wordsmith** a cover letter addressed to a specific individual, preferably the hiring managers at your targeted companies.
- **Refine** your resume and LinkedIn profile. Make sure it is written specifically for the jobs that you are applying to at these targeted companies.
- **Anticipate** questions you might be asked in an interview.
- **Write** out answers to interview questions you might be asked.
- **Roleplay** different interview scenarios so you're better prepared for whatever the hiring manager prefers. It could be a real-time online video like Zoom or Microsoft Teams or Skype. Or maybe you have to submit self-recorded video responses to random questions selected by the Human Resources Department. Maybe you'll be invited to have a face-to-face interview. That would be ideal. Promise me you will not fly by the seat of your pants for any of these potential opportunities. Any of these are your chance to strut your stuff and show off your SATs. Please do not

"wing it" because you will surely get your wings clipped. THAT will sting. Don't do it. Roleplay. Practice. Practice again. And again. You won't regret it.

Sometimes the activities above are easy to do, require little or no effort, and are pretty much not life-threatening. But other times these are things that you might not have done, or worse, don't want to do. Hold that thought.

GET OUT OF YOUR COMFORT ZONE

We're going to do an experiment, but to reap the benefits from it you'll have to put your book down. But I have to describe the experiment before you do that. So read this passage that describes the experiment, put down your book, and try the experiment.

First, fold your arms. If you're like me your **right forearm** will come to rest over your **left forearm** while your **left hand** will come to lightly envelop your **right bicep**. Otherwise, if you're not like me, your <u>left forearm</u> will rest over your <u>right forearm</u> and your <u>right hand</u> will land over your <u>left bicep</u>. For this first phase of the experiment, it doesn't matter whether your left or right forearm is on top. There is no right or wrong way to do this. No pun intended.

Now unfold your arms, drop your arms to your sides, and fold your arms again. If you're like most people, your forearms and hands ended up in the same positions as they did on the first arm folding. You could probably keep your arms crossed in this position indefinitely. It's comfortable, it doesn't hurt you, and it is not a threat to your health or well-being. Folding your arms like this is a no-brainer. You don't have to think about it or expend any unnecessary energy to accomplish this simple task. You could fold and unfold your arms until the cows come home.

Here comes the fun part: Unfold your arms one last time and drop them to your sides. Now fold your arms but switch the placement of your arms and hands compared to the way you did it before. So *left forearm* over *right forearm* if you initially did *right forearm* over *left forearm*. Or *right forearm* over *left forearm* if you initially did *left forearm* over the *right forearm*. I'll wait…

It's likely you're going to need time to accurately fold your arms in this new configuration—more time than you'd think you would need. But once you're done, chances are great you'll be uncomfortable and maybe feel slightly off balance. You'll feel slightly awkward. Uncoordinated. Definitely uncomfortable.

Here's the thing: You are safe. You are not in danger. But you ARE out of your comfort zone. And you are probably not happy to be in this awkward and uncomfortable condition. You want to get back to feeling safe, secure, and comfortable. Okay, your wish is my command. Unfold your arms.

We go through this exercise because I want you to feel how doing something you're not used to doing is something that you can do nonetheless—even if it makes you uncomfortable. You might be afraid you'll fail. You might not even know what to do or how to do it. You might be afraid you'll get hurt, rejected, or both. But you'll be no worse for the wear when you're done.

I saw this on a poster in a fourth grade classroom, FOURTH GRADE!:

**Don't Decide You Can't
Before You Discover That You Can!**

Thomas Edison, my hero, put it this way: "If we did all the things we are capable of, we would literally astound ourselves."

So if you want to successfully find your next job, you are going to have to do things you might not have done before. You might have to do things you don't know how to do initially. Find someone who can teach you. You might be uncomfortable. You'll be okay. You might stumble. You'll be okay. You might not get it right, whatever right is. You'll be okay. Fall down five times. Get up six. Get up. You'll be okay.

Over time you will overcome your hesitancy to do what must be done. Every expert was a beginner.

DOLDRUMS BEGONE!

My bad days last no more than twenty-six minutes; that's how long it takes me to watch an episode of *Frasier* on YouTube. But that's it. One episode. Not twenty-six episodes. One. Sometimes I just need to watch a few scenes and forgo the rest of the show. No matter how bad my day is going, *Frasier* snaps me out of my doldrums and sets me back on track.

Doldrums are very bad when you're looking for work. Your attempts to secure employment will be jeopardized by the negative effects of sadness and suffering. The despair you feel will creep into the letters you write, the phone calls you make, the conversations you have. You'll come across as a Debbie Downer or Toxic Tony. No one will want to be around you or help you. Who would want to hire you? Who would want to bring you into their positive and upbeat circle for you to bring it down? I wouldn't. Would you? Be a Positive Paula! A Jovial Jimmy!

So what do you do to turn your bad day into a better day? What do you do to get out of your doldrums? I usually ask those questions during my seminars to see what others do to reverse those effects of dreariness and despondency.

The following is a random collection, listed in no particular order, of some of the responses I've received over the years. Perhaps there is an activity below that you can do to help you overcome those moments when you need a break. One activity, maybe two. You can certainly try all of them, just not on the same day. Remember, you're taking a break. You are NOT looking for an excuse to stall your job search. Right? Right!

DOLDRUMS-FIGHTING TACTICS AND ACTIVITIES (LISTED IN NO PARTICULAR ORDER)

- Sew.
- Play with my kids, grandkids.
- Talk with my spouse, partner, or significant other.
- Do jigsaw puzzles.
- Walk.
- Read a novel.
- Knit.

- Call a friend or relative.
- Work in my garden.
- Sing.
- Journal.
- Lift weights.
- Cook.
- Read a magazine.
- Write.
- Surf.
- Nap.
- Bake.
- Jog.
- Declutter a drawer, shelf, closet, room.
- Run.
- Clean something.
- Quilt.
- Watch a movie.
- Swim.
- Bicycle.
- Play with my pets.
- Ice skate.
- Dance.
- Listen to music.
- Run.
- Write a song or poem.
- Go to the beach.
- Solve a crossword or Sudoku puzzle.
- Get a massage.
- Play a musical instrument.

- Kayak.
- Volunteer at a soup kitchen, assisted living facility, church, synagogue, youth group.
- Take a hot bath.
- Meditate.
- Keep a success journal.

Using this list as a guide, you would be hard-pressed not to break out of any doldrums that come your way during your job search. I'm not a healthcare professional but I'm sure if you asked one, they would say taking a break is critical to help you maintain your sanity and overall health. Since you are a human, not a machine, you cannot nor should not look for work 24/7. That is insane and just not sustainable.

Try some of these activities that your fellow job seekers have shared when you need to step away from the grind. I'll admit I don't do all the items on the above list, but I do one of them every day without fail, and I am not ashamed to lay it on the table here for you to bear witness. It rejuvenates me and recharges my battery.

I nap. Every day.

Usually in the afternoon. Usually after I've eaten something—heavy or light it doesn't matter. Usually anywhere I can sit, rest my head, and zone out.

In my car at a rest stop on the Garden State Parkway or a service road off the Long Island Expressway or an exit off the Belt Parkway. At the library. At a doctor's office while waiting for my appointment. I think eating triggers my body and mind to shut down temporarily. No. I KNOW the eating triggers my nap. I don't fight it.

I set the alarm on my phone for ten to twenty minutes, depending on how much rest I feel I need. I know it's coming so I let the feeling overtake me but only after I know I'll be safe (not a good idea to nap while driving!) and that others around me will be safe, too (again, napping and driving are not a good combo).

I get comfortable, support my head so there are no sudden jerky reactions as I nod off, close my eyes, and succumb to that glorious feeling of peace and tranquility. When the alarm sounds, I almost always wake up out of an amazingly deep sleep, then need a few seconds to catch my bearings and remember where I am. It's the best!

If you don't nap during your day, you are missing out on a fantastic opportunity to recharge and rejuvenate yourself. In your attempt to sell yourself on your job search, feeling revived and invigorated trumps tired and fatigued any day. If one of the activities on the list builds you up and gets you out of your doldrums, go for it. Otherwise, may I suggest a daily nap? Just saying.

ACTION ITEMS

- Start and maintain a **Success Journal**. Keep track of the small successes you have every day. The lead you were given. The phone call you had to gather information about a company or hiring manager. The cover letter you wrote or revised. Any changes you made to improve the strength of your resume. The networking Zoom call you participated in. The new LinkedIn connection you made. Over time your journal will start to fill with these small successes.

- When you find yourself heading into the doldrums of despair and are about to have a bad day, open your success journal to any page and start reading about positive things you've done. Before long your bad day may not feel so bad anymore, at least it may not get worse. Try it.

- Add your own items to the list of Doldrums-Fighting Tactics and Activities.

- Watch the movie *Miracle on Ice* for a better understanding of discipline and how you have to do what you don't want to do if you want to have what you want.

- **Don't paint your kitchen!**
- **Don't paint your kitchen!**
- **Don't paint your kitchen!**

CHAPTER 15
HANDLING OBJECTIONS

Every sale has five obstacles: no need, no money, no hurry, no desire, no trust.

—*Zig Ziglar*

Obstacles are the things that show up as you pursue your goals. They effectively are distractions, usually showing up unannounced and at the worst possible times. If they could speak they would tell you they're not interested in your objectives—they are only interested in your attention and keeping you from achieving those objectives. Obstacles lie in wait ready to make you take your eyes off the prize. Refer back to the discussion about drive and football players for a refresher on obstacles and why they have to be nipped in the bud.

When it comes to selling, some of the obstacles you face come in the form of objections. Objections can be either expressions of disapproval or they can be reasons for arguments presented in opposition.[7] These expressions or

---

[7] Dictionary.com; Merriam-Webster.com.

arguments are an inherent component of the sales process. Rarely, an objection doesn't rear its ugly head during a sales pitch or presentation. Every successful salesperson knows this and prepares for it accordingly. In anticipation of getting pushback from a prospect or being presented with an expression of disapproval, successful salespeople catalog the typical objections that might get tossed in their path.

Contrary to popular belief, there is a limited number of such objections. According to Zig Ziglar, there are at least five—and they are industry agnostic. Regarding your job search, I'm sure you've heard the same three to five objections that are variations of those on Zig's list.

As a job seeker, you can increase your chances of landing your next job by thinking through the objections you might receive from hiring managers. But you might win the grand prize if you continually practice rehearsing well-thought-out and carefully crafted responses that you then deliver with unwavering confidence and conviction.

If you're an older worker as we've discussed earlier in the book, you've probably been told you're overqualified, your salary requirements are too high, or you'll leave as soon as a better offer comes along. Sheesh! If you're brand new to a job search or a younger worker, you've probably heard you don't have enough experience. Yuck! And if you're considering reentry into the job market, I suspect you've been told you're out of sync with the world or some derivation thereof. Ugh!

With those possible objections to consider and prepare for, you should figure out how to drive around, over, or through those roadblocks. Rehearse ad nauseum so you can allay the hiring prospects' fears and calm their nerves. Some salespeople write out their comebacks and wordsmith incessantly until their retorts flow like melted chocolate in a chocolate fountain that you'd see at the dessert table of a lavish wedding.

You should consider doing the same. No, not go to a wedding and dip strawberries in chocolate! Although the thought of that does seem enjoyable. You should anticipate the objections you're likely to receive. Prepare responses and rehearse your delivery. If you're answering via the written word, make sure your response is direct, focuses on the objection, and is grammatically correct. If you're in an interview, you still want to be direct and focused, but now you also have to sound eloquent. That eloquence comes from you practicing in a friendly, nonhostile environment long before you're actually in the interview. You must sound confident and appear neither undeterred nor shaken. You do NOT want to stumble your way through an interview as you tackle the hiring prospect's objections.

Be prepared. Remember, if you wing it at this stage of your job search, you will get your wings clipped. OUCH! Don't say I didn't warn you.

COLLECTING NOS

Successful salespeople measure their progress toward their goals by tracking discrete, quantifiable outcomes such as the number of:

- Prospects called
- Prospects spoken to

- Appointments created
- Client meetings held
- Sales dollars generated

For you, the job seeker, those metrics might be the number of:

- Companies researched
- People you contacted in your network via phone, mail, or email
- Requests you've made for informational interviews
- Jobs you've applied to
- Cover letters you've written that were accompanied with a resume
- Rejections

That last one hurts but it is critical you track rejections if you want to land your next job. Why? Because studies have shown that when it comes to selling products and services, it sometimes takes seven to ten touches for a customer to acknowledge a salesperson and/or their offer. Seven to ten times! Not one or two.

Seven to ten touches in any combination are sometimes required for a customer to even acknowledge and/or react to a salesperson. A touch can be defined as a phone call, a letter, a postcard, a handshake at a business event, an email, a FedEx or UPS overnight letter or package, or a greeting in the street. There are probably others you can think of and include in your job search. Any combination will do. In any order. But if you believe in the data, you need seven to ten touches to improve your success rate.

Now there's no guarantee that seven to ten touches will do the trick. No guarantee. But if the evidence is real, is it any wonder that after sending in only one cover letter and resume you're not hearing back from a hiring manager? You have to reach out and touch them. Often. How often? Glad you asked. Seven to ten times. You have to follow up. The science makes it clear, and the results are irrefutable.

Let me put it this way: If you don't, someone else will or is doing so right now. Now they might not be successful, but they certainly have a much better chance of getting through and hitting the jackpot than you do. Do you see that?

What you have to do, and what successful salespeople thrive on, is to collect Nos so you can get to your Yes. Every No gets you one No closer to Yes. You almost have to feel relief when you get a No and gratitude for the rejection. Huh? Wait. What!?

Yep. Collecting Nos eliminates all the hiring managers who are not interested in you. The hiring manager that rejects you is letting you off the hook. She is telling you to continue to search somewhere else. She is saying don't wait for me to call you because I won't. She is effectively permitting you to seek out your next job. To paraphrase Southwest Airlines' tagline: "You are now free to move about the job market." Do you see THAT? You better.

It's critical to your success in finding your next job—and your mental health and well-being. Otherwise, those rejections will claw at your soul and eat up your self-esteem. Don't let that happen. You need to be strong and resilient. Remember what we discussed at the beginning of the book—hiring managers don't care about you. They're swamped and up to their eyeballs in alligators.

There is a way you can combat those rejections and get through the pain and heartache of not being wanted. When we discuss this topic during my seminars, I show the audience a simple tool that successful salespeople use to track the Nos they collect in their quest for that proverbial Yes. It's a table made up of rows of boxes, each containing an "X" except for the very last box at the end of the very last row. That box contains a big bold checkmark. That's the Yes.

The Yes can be:

- An ok for an appointment to discuss an offer
- The agreement from a client to go ahead with a
- project
- A signature to ship products or begin services

The Yes is anything positive that moves the sale along to its final destination. In your case, it could be getting the interview or landing your dream job. You decide. But you've got to track and collect Nos. It's imperative.

Now as you collect your Nos you begin to populate the table with Xs, starting with the first box in the first row. Not: no responses. No responses do not count in this process. Only Nos warrant an "X" on this table. As the Nos amass, so do the Xs. As they fill your table across the first row and continue toward your checkmark in the lower right-hand corner, you get an excellent visual of where you've been and where you're going. An excellent visual indeed!

At this point when I show the audience the graphic above, I ask if it's reasonable to expect in a job market, as you look for work, that you'll receive no more than five Nos before you get a Yes. Although there's usually one stalwart that believes it's possible (hats off to Positive Peter), practically everyone agrees that's unrealistic.

I then show the next table and ask if receiving twenty or more rejections is more in line with what a job seeker can expect to face as they climb their Mount Everest. Now a few more people join Positive Peter's party, but the majority still sheepishly shake their heads in agreement. If I look closer I sense a little anguish as well.

X	X	X	X	X
X	X	X	X	X
X	X	X	X	X
X	X	X	X	X
X	X	X	X	✔

After I let this feeling of frustration settle over the crowd and the grumbling comments subside, I then drop the bomb and show the crowd this:

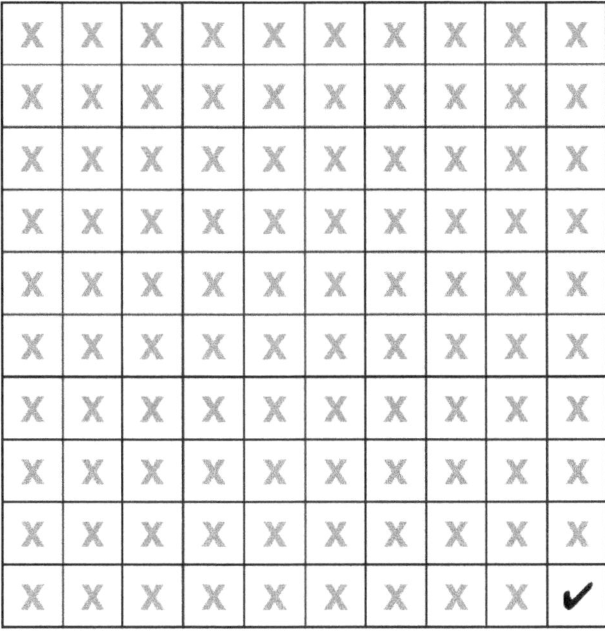

If I didn't have everyone's attention up to this point, now I have a captive audience. And those faces showing shock and disgust are now replaced by what can best be described as deer caught in headlights.

This is reality. This is what you should expect lies before you as you seek your next job. If you get there sooner, so much the better. I'd even go out on a limb to state that you probably will get your Yes long before you collect almost 100 Nos. Keep that thought in the deep recesses of your mind, though. Like most anything frightening, threatening, and overwhelming, plan for the worst while you hope for the best.

Getting into this mindset will better prepare you for the road ahead. Collecting Nos becomes your marching orders so rejections won't knock you off your feet or clip you at your knees. You'll brush away those emails that say thanks but no thanks so you can remain focused on the task at hand—collecting Nos to get to your Yes. You have to do this. Have I mentioned that enough?

Here's a picture of the chart I used for two separate job searches. I taped a piece of graph paper inside the front cover of a spiral notebook. The searches yielded twenty-three and thirty-four rejections, respectively. Note the highlighted checkmark in the lower right-hand corner. That was the Yes I was working toward. Luckily, I didn't need to collect all the rejections to completely fill the chart. Phew! Hopefully, you won't either!

ACTION ITEMS

- Create a chart so you can track rejections as you collect Nos. Put a checkmark in the lower right corner to signify your destination. Your Yes. Populate the chart as you receive rejections. No responses do not count as rejections. You must collect Nos. You have to receive rejections if you want to get to your Yes.

CONCLUSION

I'm going to get a little deep and philosophical. Please bear with me because I am trying to make an important point and believe this is a good way to do that.

There is a space between stimulus and reaction. That's what Dr. Viktor Frankl believed and how he says he was able to survive as a prisoner of the concentration camps during World War II.

In his famous book *Man's Search for Meaning*, Dr. Frankl suggests that the space between stimulus and reaction is where, and how, concentration camp survivors dealt with their circumstances—by using their power to choose their response.

While our pride may be shattered and our dignity dragged through the mud, our thoughts remain ours and cannot be taken away—unless we allow them to be taken away. According to Dr. Frankl, in our response lies our growth and freedom.

I am not suggesting your job search equates to the experience of someone interned at a concentration camp. Not even close. I am suggesting your response to the circumstances that have you looking for your next job— new to the job market, trying to get back into the job market after being let go, or reentering the job market after an extended period of time away—is in your control. Totally. Completely. You are in charge. What happens to you pales in comparison to how you react to it.

Let me ask you: When you get cut off on the highway while driving at seventy miles per hour, do you curse the reckless, apparently absent-minded driver who cut you off? Or do you speed up to catch up to them and wave at them—not with all five fingers but only your longest one? Do you pull up dangerously close behind, tailgate, and flash your high beams relentlessly to get their goat? Worse yet, do you speed up, catch up, then tailgate, flash your high beams relentlessly, AND follow them home? Into their driveway? With your horn blasting for the added measure so all the neighbors can hear you, too? Or are you grateful that no accident ensued, and that no one got hurt? Hmmm….

Or how about this scenario: You're getting ready to leave to go outside, open the door, and are surprised to see that it's raining. Is your immediate reaction: "Dang, I hate the rain?" Or did you go to school in Buffalo as I did and say to yourself, "I'm glad it's raining and not snowing?" Do you think, "Ugh, what an ugly day this is?" Or do you think, "Man, if I was an umbrella salesperson, this is gonna be a beautiful day!" Hmmm….

Let's keep going. Did you know there are people, maybe you or someone you know, who hate that roses have thorns? They just hate roses for that! They can't get it out of their heads that such beautiful flowers have spiny and painful finger-sticking devices. Meanwhile, some people love that thorns have roses. Which camp do you belong to?

Hmmm….

Last example, and this is one of my favorite stories when it comes to validating Dr. Frankl's mantra. There is a town where no one wears shoes. Two shoe salespeople are dispatched to the town to sell shoes from their extensive product line. The first salesperson returns to headquarters all discouraged and bent out of shape. "No one wears shoes in that town! What a bust! What a wasted day!" Meanwhile, the second salesperson can't contain their enthusiasm as they rush back to headquarters grinning from ear to ear. "No one wears shoes in that town! It's a gold mine! We're gonna break all kinds of sales records!"

The same set of circumstances. Totally and completely different responses.

As you search for your next job, which salesperson are you? The first one who doesn't see the forest because the trees are in the way? Can you not see the countless opportunities around you to better your life? Do you believe the world owes you a job? Hmmm….

Or are you the second salesperson, open to dealing with what's sitting in front of you? Ready to play the cards you've been dealt? Grateful for the opportunity to serve others? Up to the challenge to help the world by contributing your skills, abilities, and talents? Hmmm….

I suggest you be the second one. I suggest changing your attitude from no way to yes way. I suggest you'll dramatically improve your chances to land your next job if you take on the role of helper, servant, and solution provider.

Just like Glenda the Good Witch told Dorothy, you always had the power to go home. Use your power to choose your reaction to your circumstances. That's what Dr. Frankl would tell you to commit to. Let his first name remind you to be the victor, not the victim. Take the bull by the horns and be proactive. Incorporate the tips and techniques discussed in this book to guide and direct you as you sell yourself and land your dream job.

Good luck!

APPENDIX

(Where authors put stuff when they're not sure where they belong, but don't want to exclude them from the book)

I've discussed the following topics with my audiences over the years. I keep them in my back pocket for filler whenever someone asks a question or brings up a topic that's tangential to what's being bantered about at the moment. I could probably write a book about each of them and provide more detail about all of them. In fact, I'm sure several authors have done that already.

So I'd like to provide the following thoughts and ideas, listed in no particular order, to assist you in your job search. These are suggestions for your consideration and offered as additional tips and techniques to help you tell the world about yourself to help you find your next job.

Remember, we're counting on you to sell your SATs (skills, abilities, and talents). It's not 1950; they're not coming to knock on your door. You have to go to them and show them what you have to offer. Good luck!

SMILE

A smile is one of the few things you can give and keep at the same time. Think about that. Someone smiles at you. They give you their smile and keep theirs. You return the favor by giving them your smile while keeping yours.

You both gave your smiles away, and you still have them—to potentially share with others. What a concept!

Meanwhile, a possible added bonus of this exchange could make both of you feel slightly better than you did BEFORE the exchange. It's a win-win for everyone.

Now should you decide not to smile in return, they still have their smile. They keep it. A win for them—not so much for you.

Conversely, if you smile at someone and they don't reciprocate, you still get to keep your smile. A win for you—not so much for them.

The takeaway is that smiling is a good thing. Someone, somewhere, somehow, is going to benefit from it, but someone has to start the process—why couldn't it begin with you? Just saying.

OUT WITH THE OLD, IN WITH THE NEW

Do something different, involving all your senses, to shake up those old neural pathways. Stretch your imagination and open yourself up to the wonders and magnificence of the world around you. Get your brain to start dealing with changes in your environment and daily habits. Once you start, you won't look back. Consider the following:

- Take a different route to or from your home regardless of where you are. *You'll see things you might not have seen before.*

- Brush your teeth with your nondominant hand. *Your dentist will tell you that might prolong your enamel since you won't be brushing as hard.*

- Change the order of putting on your pant legs and shirt arms. *Do you think crossing your arms differently was uncomfortable? Wait.*

- Change the order of putting on your socks and shoes. *Definitely an uncomfortable and different feeling!*

- Get out of bed on the other side. *Takes some getting used to.*

- Read different books, newsletters, magazines, and newspapers. *Get ready to be humbled by so many more new thoughts and ideas and learnings.*

- Listen to different types of music. *So many genres, not enough hours in the day.*

- Eat different food cuisines. *Go ahead, explore!*

No guarantee you'll notice a difference if you do any of these different activities. Guaranteed you won't if you don't. Just saying.

SEVEN-PLUS BILLION PEOPLE PLUS AN ADDITIONAL 250 INDIVIDUALS FOR GOOD MEASURE

Since the days my boys were born, I've taught them to be nice to people. "But Dad, what if they're not nice to us?"

would come the pushback. "Then walk away, or run, from them if necessary."

Go find someone else to be nice to. There are seven-plus billion people on the planet—certainly, there is someone else you can be nice to. There's got to be someone who would enjoy meeting you, especially if you have a caring disposition and genuine desire to be friendly. And you might want to meet them as well, right?

Dear reader, you are going to meet many people from different walks of life as you search for your next job. Hold on, let me rephrase that: You *should* meet many people from different walks of life as you search for your next job. You should make the effort to broaden your horizons, step out of your comfort zone, and seek out new experiences and circles of influence. I know we're not supposed to be governed by "should or shouldn't." But in this case, I'll ask for leniency.

You have got to believe there are some people in this world, seven-plus billion for those keeping score, who can help you—who want to help you—land your next job, possibly your dream job. In fact, I'll go out on a limb and guarantee they're out there; you either have to find them or they have to find you. Now I cannot guarantee either of these scenarios will bring you success. I cannot. I can guarantee that if you don't look or make it possible for them to find you, then it won't.

The following simple seven-word phrase, repeated again and again by successful salespeople the world over, helps them when they feel as if they're climbing an insurmountable hill or fighting a battle they believe they can't win. And that's why you have to commit to memorizing this seven-word mantra. And then you have to recall it when you feel your efforts start to wane or you sense your dignity is under attack. Repeat after me:

Some will. Some won't.
So what? Next!

You should also know that everyone you meet knows at least 250 people that you do not know. Therefore, there is someone you know who knows someone you do not. And that second someone knows 250 someones that you do not know. If you stretch your imagination and think outside your comfort zone, one of those unknown someones could be the someone that introduces you to one of those other unknown someones who introduces you to the hiring manager that hires you.

Maybe. Maybe not. And that's because there is no guarantee that if you get out there and show up, that connection will occur. I guarantee if you don't, it won't. Just saying.

If you prefer symmetry and an even number of words in your mantras, then use this eight-word corollary instead:

Some will. Some won't.
So what? Someone's waiting!

Someone is waiting to meet you, learn from you, and be helped by you. What are you waiting for? Find 'em! Go!

BUILD PIPELINES BY BUILDING TRUST

Fire, Water, and Trust were hiking in the woods. They were enjoying their stroll through Mother Nature when the conversation turned toward what they would do if they got separated.

Fire said, "Look for the smoke. That's where you'll find me."

Water said, "Look for the lush green grass, bountiful flowers, and towering trees. I'll be underneath them all."

Trust said, "If you lose me don't bother looking. I'll be gone and probably won't come back."

Any successful salesperson worth their salt knows that there is strength in having a pipeline. A pipeline is the salesperson's list of potential prospects that could become raving fans. Emphasis on *potential* and *could become.*

As mentioned earlier in the book, there is no guarantee if a salesperson (the job seeker) treats a customer (the hiring manager) with dignity and respect that the customer (the hiring manager) will tell anyone about their thoughtful salesperson (the job seeker). No guarantee. If, however, that customer (the hiring manager) is mistreated in any way, shape, or form, I guarantee the salesperson (the job seeker) will be dragged through the mud. Forever. For eternity. Whichever comes first.

Trust is the one thing that a salesperson, or a job seeker, cannot take for granted. It must be maintained, preserved, and treasured above all else. Once your customer, or hiring manager, loses trust in you, you might as well go home and close the door on that opportunity. Do not pass Go! Do not collect $200. Game over. Hasta la vista, baby! Ciao! Adios! Arrivederci! Sayonara!

HEROES

Have you said, or felt, any of the following sentiments:

- I'm afraid to fail.
- I'm afraid to try.
- I lack courage.
- I'm too short.
- I'm too tall.
- I'm too skinny.
- I'm too fat.
- I'm too dumb.
- I'm too weak.
- I'm too plain-looking.
- I lack experience.
- I'm in the wrong place.
- It's the wrong time.
- What am I doing here?
- Why am I even here?
- I don't have what it takes.
- He doesn't like me.
- She's out of my league.

Seem familiar? If you're human, of course it does. Scientists tell us that the person you have the most conversations with is yourself. They also say the majority of those "discussions" are typically more negative than positive. Much more.

I'm just as guilty as having said to myself some of those things in the list above. Some. I would like to share a technique I use to help me keep those negative thoughts and ideas at bay. I hope you'll try it. This might work for you as well.

Think about the person you most admire—your hero, living or otherwise. Could be real. Could be a character imagined in literature or art. Somebody you admire and look up to with awe and reverence.

Who would you love to share a meal with? Who would you enjoy shooting the breeze with? Who has accomplished something that you would like to accomplish as well? Not necessarily replicate the outcome, but put your own spin or fingerprint on what they became or acquired or did so someone somewhere else in some future time will emulate you then like you're emulating your hero now.

I suggest you visualize this individual in your mind and converse with them as if they were at your side. Better yet, find a photo of them, print it, and carry it around with you. Pull it out when you need positive inspiration or you feel like talking with someone who could untangle you and free you from the negative weeds.

Nobody needs to know you're doing this. Your secret is safe with me. If anyone asks me about the photo you talk to periodically, I'll change the subject and steer the discussion back to Mr. or Ms. Nosybuddy. It's no one's business but your own.

When you're together with your hero, describe what you're attempting to accomplish—finding your next job. Share your plans for reaching your goal. Ask them for their suggestions as to how they might help you achieve your goal. Maybe even ask them what they would do if they were in your shoes.

Doing this exercise will get your mind focused on the task at hand—finding your next job. All of a sudden clues will emerge before your eyes and ears because you are more attuned to what's going on around you. The key to unlocking your success might be staring you in the face. The solution becomes evident because you set your mind on looking for ways and means to succeed.

I can't guarantee that your hero will have answers for you. I cannot. I guarantee if you don't ask, there won't be any. So ask. What have you got to lose? Again, it's between you and your hero. No one needs to know about your conversations.

CORNFIELDS

If I showed you a handful of corn seeds, would you be able to tell which ones would take root and grow into healthy plants? Probably not, right?

Maybe that's why cornfields are overflowing with cornstalks. I suspect that farmers also have no idea as to which seeds they have are suitable for planting. Nor do they know which seeds will get eaten by the birds, which will get blown by the wind, or which ones will take root or die off for some unforeseen genetic reasons soon after planting. So farmers inundate their fields with large quantities of corn seeds, possibly pray to the Corn Gods, plan for the worst, hope for the best, and see what the harvest brings.

I suggest for your job search that you plant as many seeds as possible. The advantage you have regarding these seeds is that you can control their chances to take root and grow. You can plant healthy seeds. One seed could be the networking event you attend. Another seed could be the person you meet at that event that you help by telling them about an opportunity you've uncovered.

Several seeds could be the grammatically correct and well-written cover letters you submit with your highly polished resume (more seeds). Other seeds could be the genuinely sincere thank you notes you send promptly after your interviews.

You can't possibly know which "seeds" will fall by the wayside or which ones will find fertile ground and grow. So manipulate the odds in your favor, and do what you can within your power to ensure the seeds you plant are good, healthy, and worthy of being nurtured, toiled, and harvested.

SPONGEBOB SQUAREPANTS

I interviewed for a position at a company in an industry I had never worked in before. When I called back a few days afterward to check on the status of my application, the hiring manager said she and the rest of her team felt I was overqualified for the job. They were concerned I would barrel over everyone and tell them how to do things. Or that I would leave after two weeks because I would be bored out of my mind.

Although I was taken aback initially, I replied, "Thanks, but I've never worked in this industry. You've been here forever. How could I possibly tell you how to do what you do? Hire me, and for the first month or so I'll be a sponge, absorbing as much as I can, and I'll keep my opinions to myself. When our honeymoon is over, please allow me to ask on an as-needed basis, "Why do you do things that way? Have you considered other options?"

Well, they hired me and, as promised, I listened intently, watched as much as I could with keen vision, kept my mouth shut whenever necessary, and developed writer's cramps from all the notes I took. My diligence paid off because customers appreciated my working knowledge and the information I shared with them. The management team was pleased they had an educated employee who placed a high regard on customer satisfaction.

May I suggest if you find yourself in a new position in an unfamiliar industry or situation that you consider being a sponge? I'm not suggesting you should be a wallflower if that behavior is not appropriate for your opportunity. But sometimes being a good student helps you become a better employee. Just saying.

BIRDS OF A FEATHER

For as long as I can remember, my parents drilled into my head, as well as my siblings' heads: ***Tell me who your friends are, and I'll tell you who you are.*** I've come to reframe that directive to mean: ***"You hang out with people you like because they're like you."*** Following that line of reasoning, when it comes to your job search I suggest you consider the people you hang out with, the information you take in, and the environment you surround yourself with.

I think you would agree that people who belittle your aspirations and criticize your motives are probably not your best supporters. Also, why would you subject yourself to the negative and soul-sucking drivel that's vying for your attention when there is practically unlimited positive and upbeat content that is cataloged, sequenced, and instantly available to you on YouTube and Google? Finally, immersing yourself in an unloving, noncaring, and downtrodden environment has got to have negative effects on you and your psyche, right?

Let's talk about people in your support circle first. Do those you hang with have a problem for every solution? Are they ardent disciples of Chicken Little? Do they try to convince you that the world owes you a job? That the job market is sucking wind?

People such as these, who are naysayers, think the sky is falling, or believe they're entitled and want to convert you to the House of Entitlement as well, are not good company to keep, in my humble opinion. These friends and family will discourage you from trying new things, will scare you into not wandering into uncharted waters, or will nag you by asking, "Why is it taking you so long to find a job?" These ne'er-do-wells are pushing you down or, worse, keeping you down. You'd best be served by people that pick you up and support you like a parent who teaches their four-year-old child how to ride a bike without training wheels.

Furthermore, for those of you who religiously watch the news, I'm sure you've been led to believe that CNN stands for Cable News Network. I have a newsflash for you—it means Constant Negative News.

I'm not clairvoyant but tonight at 11 p.m. when you tune into your favorite TV news program, the first four stories, in no particular order, will be about death, despair, destruction, and desolation. On the commercial breaks you'll catch your breath, but only until the anchors return to inform you about other problems, challenges, altercations, or disagreements around the world, in another part of your country, or even in your community or neighborhood.

Is it any wonder why you have trouble falling asleep after the broadcast is over and you turn out the lights? Subjecting your eyes and ears to that negativity and ultimately filling your mind with all that stuff cannot be conducive to a good night's rest.

Last, but not least, your environment. If you don't like where you are or the prevailing surroundings that make up your field of vision or what you're hearing, then you should change your environment. You CAN make the necessary changes to improve your chances of finding your next job. Eliminate things that detract from your mission or add things you need and are missing.

Or you can move. Physically. Move. Face it. You are not a tree. Unless you are being held against your will, pick yourself up and remove yourself from where you are, and plop yourself somewhere else. Ideally, it will be a place that cultivates growth and expansion populated with people who are upbeat, caring, empathetic, and supportive. THAT has got to have positive consequences for you and your job search. Just saying.

MIRROR, MIRROR, ON THE WALL

Suppose you're asked at an interview why you want to leave your company for a new position. I hope the following responses don't describe any or all your responses.

- You rant about your current manager in a not-so-positive vein.
- You trash the lackluster performance of your company.
- You take pleasure in chastising your colleagues and criticizing their work ethic.
- You have to get off your chest how poorly you are treated.

Even if your manager is not so nice or your company is subpar in any number of metrics or your coworkers are not ideal models of efficiency and effectiveness or your working conditions are not so great—who made you the judge and the jury? This is a good time to remember your mother's timeless advice: If you have nothing nice to say, don't say anything.

Regardless of who or what you target in your response to what seems like an innocuous question, your words, temperament, and demeanor will be noted. Why? Two reasons. First, the hiring manager will wonder if your barbed attacks are real or imagined. Second, they'll question whether in time you'll feel the same about their beloved company and its exemplary employees.

We're taught in sales training that you're always on, even when you think you're not selling. The actions you make or don't make and the words you say or don't say are being observed and heard. Count on it. Someone's watching and listening. Clients. Competitors. Colleagues. Managers. If you've come this far with me and agree that looking for your next job is akin to selling yourself, then you're on—especially at your interview. Especially. You are always on.

So if that's true—trust me, it is—imagine that your face-to-face interview takes place in a room with a rather larger than normal mirror on the wall facing you. You've seen enough police dramas to know that there are probably people on the other side of that piece of glass. They are observers who are taking in this exchange between you and the hiring manager. Their opinions are highly regarded, and they will influence any hiring decisions.

Now stretch your imagination and pretend you're one of the observers with them behind the glass. You are watching and listening and taking in all that is happening between you and the hiring manager seated across the table from you. Really observing. Really listening. Really taking it all in. Would you hire you? Hmmmm….

AND THE *FILL IN THE BLANK* GOES TO…

If you ever watch an award ceremony such as the Emmys, Grammys, Oscars, Tonys, Country Music's CMAs, Espys, whatever, you know you can count on the following:

Winners will come on stage and accept their award. They will thank the award-giving organization for the wonderful recognition and honor. They will scour the room and make eye contact with their fellow nominees, then thank them and say how humbled they are to even be included with them in whatever category they're in. They'll thank their support team, maybe their kids, possibly their parents.

We've grown accustomed to this script and expect it to play out as each winner traipses across the stage and our screens.

But I bet dollars to donuts—I still don't understand what that means!—that in any of those ceremonies, one winner will deviate from that script. Before, during, or after their acceptance speech, they will stare right into the camera with steely eyes—maybe even teary eyes—take a deep, deliberate, and prolonged breath, and say with conviction something that sounds like this: "If you're out there debating whether you should continue with your practice routine and sacrifice for what you truly believe in, let me assure you that you should. People told me I was crazy. Others said I was wasting my time. Well, I'm living proof that all the blood, sweat, and tears will be worth it when you receive this award. So stay the course, remain focused, ignore the naysayers, be diligent, and summon all your strength, courage, and discipline so that one day you can be here on this stage and accept this award."

My dear reader, if you take the time to go through the process to establish the dream job you want and plow ahead and do all you're supposed to do to get the job offer you desire, then I suggest you follow that award winner's advice and do what you have to do so you can "accept that award."

YOU MUST DO THIS

It's only fitting that we end with the following discussion. If you set aside your identity as a job seeker and take on the role of a salesperson in your quest to find your next job, if you do your personal assessment to determine what your next career move is, if you research companies, if you write convincing cover letters and submit them with noteworthy resumes, if you have interviews due to all your hard work and effort and like what you hear and see in those interviews, if you see yourself working for any of these companies, then I hope you do the one thing that many job seekers don't do—you MUST ask for the job offer.

It's what salespeople colloquially refer to as asking for the business—or closing. Closing is a misnomer because you're not closing the deal but rather opening the door to a new relationship and potential for future growth. If you don't ask for the job offer, how will they know you want it?

Ask for the job offer. Tell them you enjoyed the conversation and loved what you heard about the company and the position. Hopefully, they enjoyed meeting you and learning more about you as well.

Ask what other information they need from you to help them make their decision. If you're so inclined, you could ask them when they would like you to start. That's bold but why not!?

Afraid to do this? Roleplay the scenario. Practice asking. Hear yourself asking for the job offer. Figure out how you will ask for it. Have your practice partner assume different temperaments for when you ask for the offer. Play out different responses to your request for this fantastic job from "Excellent! We'll send you an offer via email tonight." (*Yeah, baby!*) to "We have to talk among ourselves before we can make a decision." (*Ok, you're still in the running*) to "No, we don't think you're a good fit for us." (*Uh-oh, but still good to know.*)

Practice in a friendly, nonhostile environment where you can make mistakes and tweak responses. Doing so will help bring into formation all the butterflies that are circling in your stomach. Do it before you walk into your interview. A lot. Remember, if you wing this step in the process and fly by the seat of your pants, you could get the seat pulled out from under you and your wings clipped. Pain, rejection, AND dejection all in one fell swoop! Ouch!

Now there's no guarantee if you ask for the job they will make an offer. No guarantee. I guarantee if you don't ask they probably won't. Maybe they will. Don't know. Who does? So stack the odds in your favor, and guide the discussion in your direction.

What have you got to lose? A job you never had? Uh, you never had it. What have you got to gain? A job you want? Hmmmmmm……

RESOURCES

Allen, James: *As a Man Thinketh*
Nuggets of gold are strewn across the pages of this cerebral treatise on how we become what we think about. Interesting concepts that could, and should, change the way you think.

Bolles, Richard Nelson: *What Color is Your Parachute?*
The undisputed champion in the self-help section of your local bookstore for helping individuals decide what they want to be when they grow up—or at least the things they could do until they figure it out. Sound familiar? Can you relate?

Buckingham, Marcus: *Go Put Your Strengths to Work*
Surveys of tens of thousands of people, just like you and me, are used to assess what fills us up with pleasure and contentment as well as what drains the life out of our souls and depletes our energy reserves.

Carnegie, Dale: *How to Win Friends and Influence People*
Your world will change (*at least people will think you're nicer than you were, and you'll think people are nicer, too*) but only if you practice the time-tested advice doled out by Mr. Carnegie.

Dweck, Carol: *Mindset*
Your level of success you attain is usually a function of your mindset…or lack thereof.

Helmstetter, Dr. Shad: *What to Say When You Talk to Your Self*

Need help to keep that negative voice in your head in check? Look no further than this great read for assistance in taming the savage beast.

Hill, Napoleon: *Think and Grow Rich*

There are no secrets to attaining success. No need to recreate the wheel. You can find your cheat sheet in this best-selling book that highlights the personality traits and business acumen of 500 of Andrew Carnegie's most successful and accomplished friends.

Maltz, Dr. Maxwell: *Psycho-Cybernetics*

Who would have thought that a plastic surgeon could uncover clues about his patients' trials and tribulations? You'll find many tips and techniques for managing your internal board of directors while raising your self-esteem to levels you didn't think possible, and that others will notice as well.

Mandino, Og: *The Greatest Salesman in the World*

Don't let the title scare you. If you breathe, you should read this book. Enough said.

Packard, Dave: *11 Simple Rules*

Proof that you don't need a lot of rules, or words, to demonstrate compassion and concern for others.

Piper, Wally: *The Little Engine That Could*
Compared to the other resources in this list, this classic children's book should take about ten minutes to read, fifteen if you take the time to enjoy the colorful illustrations. Now that you're an adult, pay special attention to its message. Then say to yourself, "Yes! Yes, I can!" And again. And again. And again.

ACKNOWLEDGMENTS

The Career Forum at the Somerset Y, specifically Bob, Lloyd, and Denis, are indirectly responsible for helping me get here. They supported my efforts to share my engineering and sales background with unemployed professionals seeking guidance in their job search. Because of these three, I had the opportunity to facilitate countless seminars at the Y and extrapolate my experience and expertise to lead discussions about selling yourself in the job market. Thank you, gentlemen!

I know what I don't know, and the team behind the scenes of this book brought all the unknowns to the forefront. Their collective efforts helped to create this finished product so that in the end it looks like I know what I'm doing! Thank you, Vivian, Laura, and Eric. An extra special thank you to the conductor of our ensemble for knowing who should do what, when, and why. Karen, thank you for all your help, support, guidance, suggestions, direction, and advice. Not necessarily in that order.

Mom and Dad, strange, isn't it? Each person's life touches so many other lives. When they're not around, they leave an awful hole, don't they? I'm having a wonderful life! Thank you!

To my grandparents, aunts, uncles, and cousins (with us or in our memories) strewn across the country and around the world in Montevideo and Buenos Aires, I hope I've made you proud.

Rosie and Mike, supportive siblings, even though I might not reciprocate as much as I should.

To my sons Jared and Josh, without you tomorrow wouldn't be worth the wait, and yesterday wouldn't be worth remembering.

To Caryn, Katie, and Justice for taking care of the important men in my life, who I trust are taking care of these important women as well.

To Lisa for encouraging me to be tenacious and resourceful, pushing me to step out of my comfort zone and guaranteeing I'm not the smartest person in the room when I'm with you.

Jon, gone too soon. I feel your presence every day. Your friendship is eternal. I wish you could have been here with me to see this through to its completion—in some strange, spiritual way you have been. And Sherri, a rock and constant source of support and encouragement.

To the moderators of the many networking groups I've had the pleasure of working with over the years. Your kindness and support have made it possible for me to be in front of people who I would not have had the opportunity to meet otherwise. Thank you!

Finally, to the countless job seekers I've had the pleasure of meeting and coaching over the years. I always look forward to facilitating conversations about helping you get from where you are to where you want to be. Those who have seen me in person or on-screen will attest to my upbeat and positive mental attitude. While your newfound enthusiasm for what we discuss encourages you to journey on with your job searches, your energy and excitement fill me with joy and inspiration and makes me feel like I'm floating on air. The adrenaline rush fires me up so much that I want to continue sharing the tenets of selling yourself all day long, day after day. Just saying. Thank you, and good luck in your quest to find your dream job!

ABOUT THE AUTHOR

Joey Himelfarb has been selling, training, and serving clients for over twenty-five years.

He studied physics and mechanical engineering. He began his career working on the installation of trans-oceanic fiber optic telecommunications cables around the world. He was chosen to teach his colleagues and clients the fundamentals of fiber optic technology; some say that is where, and how, he began his sales career. Since then he has sold in a range of industries including automotive, home improvement, and training and education. Whether it's with multimillion-dollar Fortune 100 companies around the world or consumer products in a homeowner's backyard, Joey enjoys helping his clients get from where they are to where they want to be. He uses his problem-solving techniques to help professionals at all levels maintain a positive attitude and an optimistic approach to work and life.

Joey's passion is being on stage and encouraging people to maintain positive mental attitudes. He contends that we sell every day, and that being negative serves no function. To that end and on a regular basis, Joey leads discussions and facilitates seminars designed for job seekers, career changers, small business owners, people struggling with substance abuse and addiction, and several youth groups such as the Boys and Girl Scouts and teenage chapters of the YMCA.

Most people who have participated in these seminars have learned new tactics for selling themselves and maintaining positive mental attitudes in their professional and personal lives. Some attendees have seen and heard a unique similarity in Joey's presentation style with a famous comedian who has had success hosting several Oscar Award Ceremonies.

Joey's presentations are always thought-provoking and entertaining. Invariably, several attendees lament how quickly the time flies. In addition, they wish they could spend more time learning from this upbeat, positive, and enthusiastic speaker.

Joey is a devoted father and grandfather and an experienced athletic coach and life coach as well. Reach out to him at joey@mojoegroup.com.